Spain Is Different

The InterAct Series

Edited by
GEORGE W. RENWICK

Spain Is Different

HELEN WATTLEY AMES

INTERCULTURAL PRESS, INC.

For information, contact:
Intercultural Press, Inc.
P.O. Box 700
Yarmouth, Maine 04096, USA

Cover Design: Letterspace

Printed in the United States of America

97   5 6

Library of Congress Cataloging-in-Publication Data

Ames, Helen Wattley
    Spain is different/Helen Wattley Ames.
        p. cm. — (InterAct series ; 9)
    Includes bibliographical references.
    ISBN 1-877864-11-0
    1. National characteristics, Spanish. I. Title. II. Series.
DP52.W38 1992
946—dc20   92-28959
                                                          CIP

For my parents,
George and Margaret Wattley

Contents

IRELAND

WALES

ENGLAND

English Channel

NETHERLANDS

GERMANY

BELGIUM

LUXEMBOURG

FRANCE

SWITZERLAND

AUSTRIA

ITALY

Bay of Biscay

PYRENEES

ANDORRA

Corsica

SPAIN

Balearic Islands

Sardinia

MEDITERRANEAN SEA

PORTUGAL

Strait of Gibraltar

MOROCCO

ALGERIA

TUNISIA

La Palma

Lanzarote

Tenerife

Arrecife

Gomera

Santa Cruz

Fuerteventura

Hierro

LAS PALMAS

Gran PALMAS
Canaria

CANARY ISLANDS

CHAZAUD

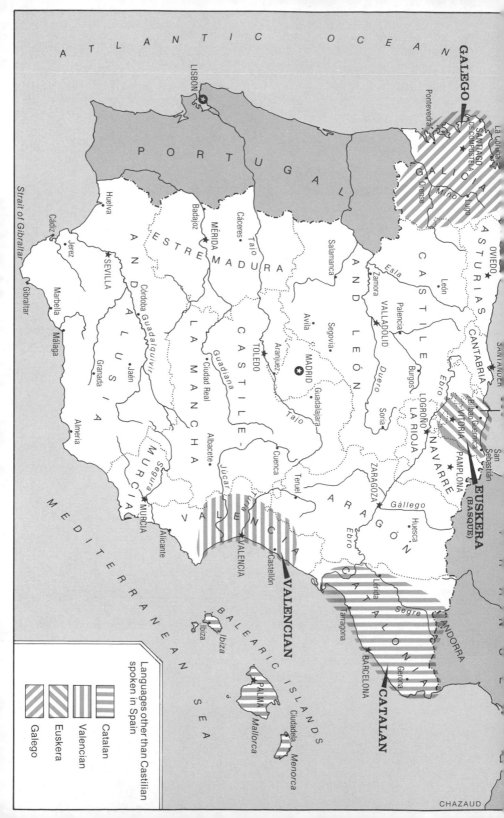

Preface

The year 1992 marks the five-hundredth anniversary of the first voyage to the New World of Cristoforo Colombo, a Genoese in the service of the Spanish crown. Commemorations of this event, along with the Olympic Games in Barcelona and the World's Fair in Seville, have focused the attention of many Americans on Spain for the first time. The significant economic development of Spain during recent years and its active participation in the European Community have also attracted new interest from American companies in a variety of industries.

Business personnel, diplomats, students, athletes and other visitors going to Spain are discovering the truth of an early slogan of the country's tourist industry: *Spain is different*. Although this phrase has sometimes been used when comparing Spain negatively with other countries, its original intention was to celebrate the special identity of Spain, its culture and its people.

In this book, a volume in the InterAct series, we focus very closely on the culture and the people and pay special attention to the particular ways in which these differ from the culture and people now dominant in the New World. This InterAct, like the others, explores the different histories through which the two peoples have lived and the distinctive values they hold. Their perceptions and expectations of each other are examined.

Different ways of thinking, acting and interacting in both social and work situations are explained. Examples are given of how words and actions of a person from one culture impress, frustrate, motivate or embarrass someone from the other. Points of potential conflict are anticipated, and specific guidelines are offered to help ensure mutual understanding and cooperation.

Our purpose is to enable each person who reads an InterAct to be more confident in approaching the foreign culture and more competent in communicating with its people. Better relationships can then be developed and major goals can be achieved. Americans who travel to the country can become more perceptive observers and respectful (as well as respected) guests. Americans who live there will be better equipped to become more successful competitors, contributing colleagues or trusted friends.

We asked our own colleague and friend, Helen Wattley Ames, to write this book because she has lived in Spain, in Barcelona, where she worked at the Institute of North American Studies from 1982 to 1987 and experienced firsthand the interaction of Spaniards and Americans. Helen is fluent in Spanish, having received her bachelor's degree in Spanish language and literature at the University of Bristol, England. She comes from Trinidad and Tobago, a country with a Spanish heritage of its own.

In preparing this book, Helen interviewed carefully selected men and women in Spain who are keenly aware of the cultural differences and difficulties between Spaniards and Americans. The chapters which follow include a combination of the insights Helen has gained from her studies, her work, and her in-depth interviews. Her explanations will clarify many perplexing situations for anyone who deals with these surprisingly divergent peoples.

George W. Renwick
Editor, InterAct series

Acknowledgments

I am grateful to all the people who answered questions and read and commented on the manuscript of this book:

Carlos Alcabés, Joan Azulay, Rick Azulay, Pedro Beltrán, José María Bonsoms, Carmen Canes, Michael Chandler, Carlos Conde, Laurie Derechin, Robert Friedman, Ron Green, Sue Hershelman, John Hunter, Nora Ligorano, Gabriel Lluch, Connie Luff, Rosa María Malet, Robert Maple, Gloria Moure, Joaquin Muns, Marshall Reese, Francisco Sánchez, Neus Silva, Mike Vaal, Enrique Vidal-Ribas and Silvia Vidal-Ribas.

The editors at Intercultural Press: Peggy Pusch, David Hoopes, Kathleen Hoopes and Judy Carl Hendrick .

Special thanks to Bill Ames for all his support.

1

Spain Is Different

What Is Spain?

Regional differences
Spain is a large country (by European standards), characterized by marked regional differences more substantial than variations in local cuisine or folk music.

Geographically, it might be said that Spain faces in four directions: toward the Atlantic, toward Europe, toward the Mediterranean, and toward Africa. The climate varies accordingly. Andalucía, in the south, has a North African climate with mild winters and extremely hot summers. The center of the country is high plateau (*meseta*) and is quite arid, with little forest cover and extreme temperature variation. The Mediterranean coast, known as *Levante*, is neither as hot as Andalucía nor as cold as the meseta. Galicia and Cantabria, in the northwest, are lush and green from the copious rainfall from the Atlantic. The Pyrenees, Spain's northern boundary with Europe, are snow-covered much of the year, and the valleys of the foothills are covered with pine forests and flowering meadows.

The regions of Spain are also historically different from one another. It is said that all the peoples of southern Europe came to Spain and stayed. To the original Celts and Iberians have been added Carthaginians, Romans, Goths, North Africans and others. Although the Moors, as North African Muslims are usually called in Spain, at one time overran almost all of the country (except the Basque areas in the north), the degree of their influence varied. Throughout Spain, architecture that bears the mark of Moorish influence can be seen, but it was in Andalucía, where they ruled for nearly eight hundred years, that the Moors left their most indelible imprint. The people, architecture and lifestyle of Andalucía are those most commonly seen by foreigners as typically Spanish. The northeastern region of Catalonia had more links with southern France and with parts of Italy. Catalonia, the Basque country, Cantabria and Galicia were the first parts of Spain to be "reconquered" from the Moors and to develop their own systems of social organization, so that the Muslim influence is much less evident there than in Andalucía.

The diversity of Spain's regions is recognized in the Constitution of 1978, in which autonomous regions were established with separate governmental and, to a certain extent, financial structures, comparable in many ways to the federal system of the United States.

In terms of identity and loyalty, consciousness of region is probably stronger in Spain than consciousness of country. In the United States national patriotism is far more important than regional loyalty because the concept of the nation was one of the links that held together a country of radically disparate peoples, spread over a sparsely settled continent. Thus, national loyalty has traditionally been a public virtue. Flags in front yards and the daily pledge of allegiance in schools are outward manifestations of a patriotism that was also given widespread public expression by such events as the 1976 bicentennial celebrations and the 1986 celebrations of the centennial of the Statue of Liberty. The 1984 Olympic Games in Los Angeles became a patriotic event to a much greater extent than in other countries that have hosted the Olympics. Finally, the 1990-91 Gulf War

(Operation Desert Shield/Desert Storm) was portrayed by the U.S. administration and media, and perceived by many Americans, as a grand patriotic achievement.

In Spain, the imposition of nationhood upon existing smaller nations has left the country with strong regional identities which have persisted despite the efforts of successive central governments to dilute them. Most recently, the Franco regime suppressed regional languages and fostered migration between regions (notably, from Andalucía to Catalonia). Further, national patriotism during the Franco era took on unfortunate connotations when it was equated with xenophobic policies or what amounted to complacent isolationism. In reaction to this recent history, regional governments now direct their efforts toward regional nationalism, especially through cultural policies that foster the language, traditions, literature and arts of the region, often to the detriment of a national perspective.

Spaniards as well as outsiders are concerned about the degree to which local governments overdo regional nationalism. Years ago, the Catalan writer Miquel Llor coined the name Comarquinal for a fictional city that represented the worst in small-minded provincialism (the equivalent of Sinclair Lewis's Gopher Prairie in *Main Street*). It is not hard to find signs of this provincialism in the attitudes of regional governments—in the policy, for example, of a major orchestra not to hire players from other regions of Spain, even if it means hiring foreigners instead.

Strong regional identities are not unique to Spain. European countries such as France, Germany and Italy also have clearly defined regional differences. Time will tell if regionalism will be diluted or strengthened by greater regional autonomy.

Language diversity

Spain is also diverse linguistically. Gallego, spoken in Galicia, is akin to Portuguese. Euskera, spoken by the Basques, is a unique language which linguists have never been able to connect to another language family. Suggested origins range from

Atlantis to the lost tribes of Israel. Catalan is the language of Catalonia, and Valencian (closely related to Catalan) is spoken in the province of Valencia.

These languages are taught in school and given equal status with Castilian—native to Castile and the official language of Spain—in the respective regions. Visitors must be ready and willing to deal with bilingualism in the people they encounter. Foreigners are not generally expected to learn the regional languages unless they settle in for a lengthy stay, but they must beware of dismissing them as dialects or of considering their use pretentious. Language is a highly sensitive and politicized issue in Spain, particularly in bilingual areas, and insensitivity can lead to trouble.

Political and social changes since 1975
It is impossible to understand modern Spain without some knowledge of the Civil War, the forty-year dictatorship of General Francisco Franco, and the transition to democratic government since General Franco's death in 1975. Spain became a republic in 1931 when the king, Alfonso XIII, "suspended the exercise of royal power" and went into exile (he formally abdicated in 1941). Social and political tensions grew along with economic problems, and the accompanying confrontations between political factions finally erupted with a military uprising in July 1936, led by Franco. This revolt was the beginning of the Civil War that lasted until 1939 and resulted in the defeat of forces loyal to the Republican government by Franco's Nationalists. It is estimated that between one and two million Spaniards died during the war, and massive destruction was inflicted upon the country. Franco became head of state and his dictatorship lasted until his death in 1975, when Spain became a monarchy once again under King Juan Carlos, grandson of Alfonso XIII. A series of transitional governments led to the Constitution and elections of 1978. Spain today is a constitutional monarchy with a national parliament and senate in Madrid as well as autono-

mous regional governments with their own parliaments.

Political feelings run deep in Spain. There are still people alive who fought in the Civil War. Many Spaniards, including Pablo Picasso, lived out their lives in other countries rather than remain in Spain under Franco. Others stayed in Spain but suffered the consequences of having been on the wrong side in the war. Some of today's prominent public figures spent time in Franco's prisons because of their political beliefs. On the other hand, many Spaniards look back with nostalgia to Franco's day, which they see (especially in retrospect) as being free from modern evils such as crime, drug abuse, AIDS, divorce and abortion. Spaniards in general are politically sensitive, and also uncomfortably aware of the fact that the restoration of democracy in Spain is recent and that its stability can be threatened, as it was in 1981 when members of the Civil Guard occupied the national parliament building in an attempted coup.

Foreigners working with Spaniards should be alert to the possibility that their Spanish colleagues may hold radically opposing political views. This is also true in the U.S. but with two important differences. First, the range of political opinion among Americans is not usually as great, so disagreement may be less extreme. Second, while Americans often separate politics from other activities ("Let's leave politics out of this"), the same is far less true of Spaniards.

Spain and Latin America: La madre patria
Ties between Spain and Latin America are strong. Columbus made landfall in the Americas in 1492, setting off a surge of Spanish conquest and settlement. Spain imposed its language, laws, architecture and culture on an empire extending from Florida to Argentina. Many Latin American nations came into being with the wars of independence from Spain in the early nineteenth century, but it was not until the Spanish-American War of 1898 that Spain lost Puerto Rico and Cuba, its last colonial possessions in the Western Hemisphere.

Diplomatic, governmental and quasi-governmental, commercial, cultural and emotional ties live on. A flood of Spanish intellectuals found refuge in Mexico after the Spanish Civil War of 1936-39, and in the 1970s Chileans and Argentinians, among others, went to Spain to escape repressive governments at home. A number of Latin American countries allow dual citizenship with Spain. Since 1975 the transition from dictatorship to democracy in Spain has been held up as a model for Latin America. The ties are such that in 1986 the Queen of Spain visited Colombia to offer Spain's sympathy, solidarity and aid after the disaster caused by the eruption of the Nevado del Ruiz volcano that buried a whole city in mud. In 1991 Spain joined Latin American countries in planning a concerted campaign to deal with the cholera epidemic in Peru. Spain's government is committed to defending the interests of Latin America before the European Economic Community in such areas as immigration and trading relationships as well as offering economic and political support for emerging democracies. The term *mother country* seems strange to Americans, who do not regard England in such terms. But *la madre patria* is a meaningful concept in Spain's relationship with Latin America.

Many Americans learning Spanish are first exposed to the Latin American variety (known, confusingly, as *castellano*). The difference between this and the Castilian of Spain is comparable to the difference between American and British English ("I say to-MAY-to and you say to-MAH-to..."). There is a perceptible variation in accent, with the most significant factor being the lisping of *z* and *c* before *e* and *i* in Castilian. This lisp, found in most of Spain, is often the object of mockery in Latin America, while Spaniards tease Argentinians for their characteristic lilting accent and *che* tag—comparable to the Canadian *eh?*—and Mexicans for their use of diminutives—for example, *ahorita* instead of *ahora* (now). But speaking Latin American castellano is not a disability in Spain. One adapts quite quickly to the few significant differences in vocabulary and pronunciation.

Many Americans associate Spanish primarily with Latin America. One American newcomer to Spain who had learned

Spanish in California and visited Mexico commented, "I can't get used to having these fair-skinned, European-looking people speaking to me in Spanish." Similarly, a common traveler's tale from Spaniards visiting the U.S. is that identifying yourself as Spanish leads people to assume you are from Latin America. To avoid this, the first thing a Spaniard must say is, "I'm European."

Spain and Europe: Africa begins at the Pyrenees
Flying to Spain from the north, one passes over the sharp, snow-covered peaks of the Pyrenees. On the other side is Spain. Even from the air, the landscape is unmistakably different. The Pyrenees are the fence between Spain and the rest of Europe, affecting even the weather and giving Spain its famous sunny climate.

"Africa begins at the Pyrenees" is an old saying still heard in Spain. It is attributed to other Europeans but is actually a bit of dark, self-deprecating Spanish humor which says much about the inferiority complex Spaniards have traditionally felt in relation to the rest of Europe and about their own sense of separateness and isolation. Several factors have contributed to the isolation and differentness of Spain.

Southern Spain was ruled by Muslims from North Africa for nearly eight hundred years, from the eighth to the fifteenth century. The surrender of the southern city of Granada, capital of the Muslim territories, to the *Reyes Católicos* (Catholic Monarchs) in 1492 finalized the unification of Spain into a single kingdom free from the Moors. This final conquest, followed by the expulsion later in the year of those Jews and Moors who refused to convert, was a triumph of militant Catholicism. This was the beginning of Spain's so-called Golden Age, which saw the beginning of its empire in the Americas and its rise to power in Europe. However, the expelled Jews and Moors took with them much of the financial, commercial and agricultural expertise of Spain, sowing the seeds of later economic decline. After 1588 and the defeat of the Spanish Armada, Spain's political power also waned. Increasingly isolated, Spain became embroiled in the Napoleonic Wars and a struggle for independence from France that left behind a hostility to the French that has continued to the present day. After its Civil War Spain was isolated again, ostracized by the European and North American democracies and cut off from many of the vital political and social changes that stirred Europe after the Second World War.

During the late 1950s and most of the 1960s large numbers of Spaniards emigrated to Germany and France as guest workers. A rising standard of living in those countries created jobs which their own nationals were unwilling to fill but which were attractive to people from poor farming and fishing villages in Spain. Some of these emigrants stayed, while many others returned to Spain with money they could never have earned at home. Exporting part of its population to serve as low-paid manual workers in more developed countries did nothing for the Spanish self-image.

In the 1960s "sunny Spain," where the weather was good and prices were low, became the prime vacation spot for northerners. Today, though prices have risen to general European levels, large numbers of Europeans still flock to Spain for vacations, and many own vacation or retirement homes there. As in similar places the world over, the vacationers remain ignorant of Spain, which is a source of irritation to Spaniards.

Somos el vagón de la cola, Spaniards can still be heard to say, meaning "We always bring up the rear." Technology, intellectual and social movements, political changes—all seemed to come from the north and reach Spain late, or never. As recently as the early 1970s bus tours were run from Barcelona to Perpignan in southern France, where movie theaters organized nonstop showings of movies that had been banned by the Spanish censors because of their political or social content. The trips to Perpignan are now history, thanks to the changes that have taken place in Spain since 1975. With regard to technology, however, entry into the European Economic Community has, at least initially, done nothing to alter the "Africa syndrome." A great number of multinational corporations exist in Spain, and more and more Spanish companies are being acquired by established northern European corporations.

Nevertheless, Spain is today coming into its own as a part of Europe (it entered the European Community in 1986). The campaign that resulted in the International Olympic Committee's decision to grant the 1992 Olympic Games to Barcelona represented a high point in the internationalization of Spain, along with the 1992 World's Fair in Seville. Other European countries are now expressing great interest in Spanish art, music, theater and literature, and this interest is actively encouraged by the Spanish government in order to counteract the image of Spain as a backward, "sun and cheap wine" vacation spot.

Spain and the United States

Historical, military and political relationship
In 1985 the state of Texas celebrated the 150th anniversary of its independence from Mexico. Like Florida, New Mexico, Arizona and California, Texas had been a part of the Spanish empire. During the early 1800s that empire began to break up, and in 1898 Spain's last New World territories were lost with the end of the Spanish-American War.

In 1936, with the outbreak of the Spanish Civil War, the U.S. once again became closely involved with events in Spain. The government of the Republic called for help, which was provided by the International Brigades recruited in various countries. From the U.S. came the Lincoln Brigade, some of whose members visited Spain in 1986 to commemorate the fiftieth anniversary of the beginning of the war.

The Franco government was diplomatically isolated by the U.S. until the 1950s, when it was formally recognized, and in 1953, Spain and the U.S. signed a mutual defense and aid treaty. Under this treaty one U.S. naval base and three U.S. air bases were established in various parts of Spain, with about twelve thousand U.S. military personnel.

The issue of the bases is tied in with Spain's membership in NATO (OTAN in Spanish). The delicacy of the issue and the multiplicity of views and attitudes in relation to it are exemplified by the Spanish Socialist party. As an opposition party, Socialist leaders were firmly opposed to NATO membership and promised a referendum on the issue if elected. When they came to power, however, while they did call the referendum, they also executed a 180-degree turn on the issue and advocated continued membership. The result of the referendum was a narrow margin in favor of NATO. Opinions in Spain about the U.S. military bases are much divided. One of the most common graffiti in Spain is OTAN No—Bases Fuera (No to NATO—Out with the bases). Those who have opposed NATO and the U.S. military bases feel that they involve Spain in the consequences of events which Spain does not determine or control. The U.S. bombing of Tripoli, Libya, in 1986 caused an angry reaction among many Spaniards, who felt that they were in the direct line of fire for reprisals, while Americans were safely ensconced on the other side of the Atlantic.

When, in contrast to the surprise bombing of Tripoli, President Bush in 1990 sought an international coalition against Iraq after its invasion of Kuwait, Spain lent its support. Regarding NATO, its evolution into a more European organization makes Spain's membership seem like a more logical extension of its membership in the European Community. Finally, the future of the remaining U.S. bases in Spain may be influenced as much by U.S. decisions to downsize its military presence abroad as by political opposition in Spain. In recent years the air bases have closed, greatly reducing the U.S. military presence.

Nonetheless, expressions of resentment toward the U.S. are still common in Spain. While Spain is not a hostile environment for Americans, Spaniards are kept aware by the news media of their position as a satellite or poor relation of the U.S.

Many Spaniards also disagree with the U.S. on its policies in

Latin America. Spain considers itself a special friend of the Latin American countries and their advocate in the international political arena and often takes a differing view from the U.S. on issues such as Cuba, the Central American peace process, and the U.S. role in Central America.

On these issues anti-American sentiment exists, especially among Spaniards who became adults in the 1960s and who passed through Spanish universities at that time. Again, this is not to say that Americans can expect open hostility, but rather that they will find among the people they meet distinct reservations about U.S. policies.

Because of the strategic position of the U.S. in world affairs, foreigners are as aware of U.S. politics as Americans (and are certainly far more aware than Americans of the politics of other countries). American politics are routinely discussed in the Spanish media. The attitude of the media varies from one newspaper or magazine to another, some being more pro-American than others. In all of them there is a certain ambivalence, composed of intense interest in things American on the one hand and intellectual anti-Americanism on the other. Generally speaking, the more left-wing the source, the stronger the disapproval of American policies and the more the U.S. is seen as an intruder or aggressor rather than as a friendly protector.

Americans usually think of the U.S. bases and troops in Europe, if they think of them at all, as a sign of American generosity and the American commitment to preserving Western democracy. It is a shock for them to see signs of hostility to the American presence in Spain and the rest of Europe, and very often they become resentful and angry as a result. They also feel personally attacked when Spaniards question them in what seems to be an aggressive way about U.S. policies and politics. Americans do not like foreigners criticizing the U.S., especially when this criticism is not based on real knowledge or experience.

The Spanish myth about American politics is that all Americans are right-wing conservatives. Whether Americans can dispel this myth depends on the Spaniard they are dealing with.

Some Spaniards are genuinely interested and are pleased to be informed or set straight on their misconceptions. Others have made a creed of a certain attitude toward Americans and are not interested in hearing anything that might change it.

Americans who do not wish to discuss politics, especially when they feel obliged to be advocates or apologists of their country's policies, can simply change the subject as politely as possible. Spaniards are courteous enough that they will not pursue the discussion. Also, Americans should remember that it is quite possible for a Spaniard to be anti-American politically and yet pro-American personally.

Americans have their own myth about Spanish politics. While they believe in constitutional government and the rule of law and the accountability of elected officials and public servants, they often doubt that these principles are an integral part of Spanish political thinking. They believe the only way the Franco dictatorship survived for forty years was with the approval, or at least acquiescence, of the Spanish people. Americans who believe this are skeptical or scornful of the democratic transition in Spain and quick to find fault with inconsistencies or backsliding in day-to-day politics. For example, Americans often interpret Spaniards' matter-of-fact acceptance of the importance of *enchufe* (contacts) as corruption and a sign of the general inferiority of the Spanish political and social systems, forgetting how often knowing someone can grease the wheels of the American system too.

Spaniards did accept the Franco regime, and traces of the old ways linger. Faults and inconsistencies exist, but Spaniards do not need Americans to point them out. Transition is a slow process, and the changing of a society is not accomplished in fifteen or twenty years. The myth of Spanish politics as a sort of banana republic of secret pacts, protectionism and oligarchy will not help Americans reach any sort of understanding of Spain.

Images

Images of the United States permeate the media of other countries to an extent that most Americans do not realize. American TV serials are sold around the world, as are American products, and have an enormous influence in conditioning what people think about Americans.

One image Spaniards hold of the U.S. is that of the Wild West. They see the Marlboro man on billboards and in magazines and movie theaters. "Bonanza" and "Little House on the Prairie" were hit TV shows. Everyone knows from watching "Dallas" and movies such as *Urban Cowboy* that real people still walk around wearing cowboy boots and ten-gallon hats, even if they have never been near a horse in their lives.

Another image is that of the Elvis era: the fifties, with huge cars, full skirts and bobby sox, and rock and roll. The appeal of this era is that it corresponds to a time when young people in Spain were much less liberated than they are today and looked to the U.S. (as represented in American movies) as the symbol of a freedom they did not have.

Gangsters and their modern-day counterparts are a vital feature of Spain's image of the U.S. Al Capone captured the imagination of Spain through movies. Even the word *gangster* has been adopted into Spanish, and *ganster* and *gansterismo* are Spanish words that refer to lawlessness and organized street crime. Americans, hearing of terrorist bombings, believe Spain to be a dangerous place, but Spaniards believe the U.S. to be far more dangerous. They think of the streets of American cities as pitched battlefields with shoot-outs on every corner. Reports of Mafia murders and movies such as *The Godfather* serve only to confirm the gangster image. Cities with skyscrapers, freeways, corners lending themselves to ambushes, and streets designed for car chases are the stuff of so many cops-and-robbers series that many Spaniards do not realize there is anything else to American life. (Spaniards, used to densely crowded cities with endemic parking problems, find it hard to believe that heroes and villains alike can always find a parking place whenever and wherever they need one.)

Because most Spanish visitors to the U.S. seldom venture beyond the major cities, their image of the U.S. is that of a vast urban sprawl. Their first destination is usually New York, followed by Florida, where they visit Disneyworld™ and Miami and see (or try to avoid seeing) the home of Julio Iglesias, the Spanish soccer star turned crooner. Rarely do tourists visit a small town or the countryside.

American movies and TV shows project an image of wealth. Movies that deal with poverty in the United States are restricted to the art movie circuit and do not usually reach general audiences. Spaniards are aware of poverty in the U.S. from newspaper articles, but this information does not offset the impression created by the lush sets of "Dallas," "Dynasty," and "Falcon Crest."

A negative image Spaniards have of Americans is that they are uncultured and unaware of anything outside their own limited experience. This myth has undoubtedly been reinforced by Americans who arrive in Europe without a shred of information about the countries where they will be living. One Spaniard told a story of an American woman he met in New York in a professional capacity. In the course of conversation she inquired, "You have a king in Europe, don't you?" Further contributing to the image of boorish Americans is the American style of doing business. The habit of going straight to the point in meetings and negotiations rather than indulging in some preliminary get-acquainted, personal conversation makes a negative impression on Spaniards, who think Americans must have nothing else to talk about.

Americans' images of Spain are often vague, tied perhaps to their memory of movies such as *El Cid* or *Man of La Mancha*, which present images of medieval exoticism in the midst of poverty and arid landscapes. Even the 1991 UNICEF book, *The Year of the Child*, selected for Spain the poorest of Gypsy children, photographed in somber black and white.

Americans confuse Spain with Latin America and therefore think of Spaniards as swarthy, Indian-looking individuals, perpetually engaged in civil wars and revolutions against dictatorships. So enduring is this confusion that tourists in Spain regularly buy huge Mexican-style sombreros, complete with pointed tops and tasseled brims. No Spaniard wears or has ever worn such a hat, though they do produce them for sale to tourists.

When Spain began to promote tourism during the 1960s, much was made of the most exotic and salable traditions: bullfighting, flamenco dancing, and ladies in frilly skirts sitting on horseback behind Latin Lovers in tight dark suits. These images are still prevalent among Americans, to the dismay of many Spaniards. Bullfighting in Spain is like hunting in the U.S.—it exists and has enthusiastic supporters but also many opponents. Nothing in Ernest Hemingway's writings on Spain, read by generations of Americans, suggests that Spaniards are ambivalent about bullfighting. Similarly, many Spaniards have no idea how to do any kind of Spanish dancing, despite a recent craze for *sevillanas* (one type of Andalucían dance); and the costume of frilly skirts and polka dots is restricted to special occasions in Andalucía.

Finally, Spain has a "fun in the sun" image that was also projected as part of the tourist campaign of the sixties and ensuing years. Sun, beaches, wine, and fiestas were the bait set to catch tourists. Countless people have visited Spain and gone no further than some beach resort, where they can function in their own language and eat familiar food. While this is more typical of English and German visitors, lots of Americans have also visited Spain and come away with memories only of good food, late nights, singing and dancing, and relaxing on the beach. Even those Americans who have served on the American bases in Spain are often aware of the country only as a place where people lack many of the American conveniences of life but know how to have fun and enjoy good food and wine. The quintessential vacation spot is Marbella, the luxury resort on the south coast where the world's dandies and millionaires go to spend their leisure time, moving from exclusive club to extravagant party or luxury fashion show and assiduously encouraging the gossip magazines of Spain and elsewhere to keep their names in circulation.

Spaniards, like other Europeans, have ambivalent feelings about American popular culture. They are distressed by the influx of hamburger chains, pop music and television programs from the U.S. (teenagers, of course, are delighted). While no educated Spaniard would admit to taking "Falcon Crest" or "Miami Vice" as a true picture of American life, the programs do project an image of the U.S. that many Spaniards love to hate.

Nevertheless, admiration for the U.S. is widespread, although it often coexists with resentment. Scholars, artists, exchange students, researchers and businesspeople visit the U.S. in large numbers every year, and many Spaniards now holding high positions once studied there. A visit to New York and California is the dream of many young people, and most of those who have been to the U.S. have fond memories of their experience.

Technology
Even stronger than worries about the influence of American popular culture are concerns about invasion of the Spanish economic scene by the U.S. As one Spanish newspaper commentator acidly remarked, "Why do people complain that the content of the programs is imported from the U.S. and insist on homegrown programs, when the equipment and the know-how are also imported?"

Spaniards regard the U.S. as a haven of know-how and technical expertise, an exporter of skills and technology to countries, such as Spain, that are less developed. Spaniards generally have a lot of admiration for American technology—in the "hard" sense of machines, techniques and products—as well as the "soft" side of technology, which is the approach and way of doing things. System, details and the handbook approach—writing everything down so that things can be done consistently in the most efficient way—are seen by Spaniards as being typically American.

Spaniards are usually willing to concede to Americans on the technical front, but Americans often have a hard time distinguishing between teaching Spaniards techniques and processes and teaching them the American way of doing things. For example, an American bank will have its own standard procedures based on American negotiating style or time management. One Spanish executive at a corporate training seminar was criticized for his speaking manner. The American seminar leader, fresh from the New York home office, found the Spaniard's oral presentations too diffuse. He tried to instill the point-by-point approach basic to American public speaking: tell them what you're going to say; say it; then tell them what you've said. The Spaniard resisted this speaking style, claiming that it was alien both to him and to his Spanish clients.

Americans often feel irritated at being brought to Spain to demonstrate something only to meet resistance from Spaniards. However, such resistance is inevitable if the American is trying to show Spaniards how to be like Americans. Most Spaniards do not wish to be like Americans; they only want to have the benefit of the know-how. Therefore, to be successful in Spain, Americans must be able to sift out technique from attitude.

While Americans are (according to Spaniards) relatively lacking in personal arrogance, they have an ingrained conviction of the superiority of things American. They tend to distrust Spanish products, from cars to home appliances, and assume that they are badly made and unrepairable. There are Spanish products, especially imitations of American products, that *are* inferior: for example, imitation Post-it™ notes that stick for only a minute and then fall ignominiously off. However, the undifferentiated assumption by Americans that everything Spanish will be shoddy is inaccurate.

Americans arriving in Spain should realize that they will be seen both as individuals and as symbols. As individuals they will be taken on their own merits. But they should not be startled if a taxidriver asks them why Americans voted for Ronald Reagan or a friend takes them to task about the American bases. The

U.S. is too powerful and its influence over Spanish life too pervasive for most Spaniards to be able to forget these touchy issues in Spain/U.S. relations. They may not be mentioned, but they are always present.

Adaptation

The principal lesson that Americans can learn from their experience in Spain, or anywhere else, lies in the area of cultural relativity. They learn that not only do other cultures do things differently, but they prefer to do them that way. Americans sometimes criticize the very things Spaniards are most proud of, such as their casual attitude toward rules and regulations. Or Spaniards may agree with Americans about a particular behavior such as their lack of punctuality but still prefer the Spanish value orientation to, in this case, time.

One would not have to look far to find countries and cultures that are more alien to the U.S. than Spain, which is, after all, a part of Western Europe, with a history that is closely linked to that of the U.S. and a worldview and social organization that are recognizably similar. Spaniards prize democracy and the rights of the individual. Spain's sense of its international role parallels that of the U.S.

Spaniards, like Americans, are proud of their achievements and have comparable ambitions and aspirations. Spaniards and Americans alike take pleasure in friends and family and enjoy sports, movies, books and music. On the cultural, educational and political levels, enough cross-pollination has taken place for many things to be familiar.

Yet the differences between Americans and Spaniards cause friction. Different concepts of time or different negotiating styles may be a curiosity or an irritation. What turns them into real stumbling blocks is when one or the other of the parties refuses to accept a different way just because it is different. Such intolerance and inflexibility lead to trouble. So do hasty and oversimplified judgments or myths, which, if based on hearsay or media images, are perhaps even more annoying than if based on personal impressions. Whatever the source, these judgments are insulting and usually resented.

It seems that in situations of conflict both Spaniards and Americans become "more so." If pushed, Americans become more rule-bound, stuffy and priggish (as Spaniards see it). Meanwhile, Spaniards become more defiant, emotional and irrational (as Americans see it).

It may seem unfair to American readers that much of the emphasis of this book is on how they can best adapt to Spain and to Spaniards. This reaction is understandable, especially since many Spaniards are no more adept at tolerating differences than are Americans. This point is made nicely by Fernando Diaz-Plaja in *The Spaniard and the Seven Deadly Sins*, his lighthearted yet scholarly portrait of his own people:

> The way to improve the Spaniard can be summed up in a possibility as simple as it is revolutionary.
> If from time to time, only from time to time, we were to believe that the other man might be right...
> And if this belief did not automatically make him odious...
> I believe that would be enough.[1]

At any rate, the outsider is the one who has to do most of the adapting, but Spaniards are traditionally tolerant, welcoming, and often admiring of foreigners and their funny ways. Furthermore, Spaniards take adaptation to Spain as a compliment. They are pleased when foreigners know Spanish, take an interest in customs and traditions, and travel around and get to know the country.

2

Individual and Society

Individualism

Any attempt to describe culture brings with it the danger of overgeneralization and stereotyping. Individual Americans or Spaniards may feel that they are not accurately described in the analyses that follow. The intent is not to deny individuality but rather to describe cultural differences.

Americans and Spaniards differ markedly in their beliefs regarding the importance of individualism and how the individual fits into society. The most visible differences are often superficial, but those that are less visible are often the most fundamental and can cause misunderstanding or friction.

Outward conformity

One superficial difference is clothing. Appropriate dress is important in Spain as it is in much of Europe. Concern goes beyond the often loose dress codes that are common in the U.S. workplace. Spaniards have dress codes for almost everything. Early on Sunday mornings many people wear jogging suits, though few of them are actually exercising. The jogging suit will be replaced later by much dressier clothes if the wearer plans to have lunch with the family or at a restaurant. Thus, jogging suits denote a particular combination of leisure and informality. Even the casual clothes of teenagers and university students are carefully considered—socks, for instance, always matching the sweater.

An American arriving in Spain is usually struck by clothing styles. People are always well dressed, frequently in the height of fashion. Many Americans find such clothes consciousness superficial, while Spaniards find informal American styles sloppy and unattractive. Americans also say that Spaniards follow clothing fashions slavishly, while Spaniards say that Americans will wear absolutely anything, whether it looks good or not.

Family
Another difference that Americans notice is the close-knit family structure in Spain. Families usually live in the same city, often in the same neighborhood, and sometimes in the same building. Family members frequently work together in family businesses, and grandparents commonly take care of babies and small children while mothers are out at work. Sunday lunch is a ritual involving the entire extended family. Young people generally live at home until their mid twenties or until they marry. There was a movement in the 1970s for young people to leave home and share apartments, but economic difficulties have discouraged this tendency. In the U.S., financial difficulties may also bring adult children back to the parental home, but such cases are still the exception to the general practice of leaving home by the end of one's teens.

Americans often wonder if this closeness with family doesn't stifle individuality in Spaniards, producing people who follow custom and tradition without question. Spaniards, on the other hand, often see Americans as rootless, cast out of the home too young, and forced to make their own way without the benefit of financial and moral support and the network of family contacts.

Perhaps the fundamental difference between Spanish and American individualism is that for an American, personal individuality or independence is a state of mind and source of identity as well as a lifestyle. For Americans, the Spanish way, which seems to subordinate individuality to social appearances and family loyalty, must result in a loss of personal identity. Spaniards, however, don't see it that way.

For Spaniards, the family constitutes the kind of social and economic support system that many Americans would be inclined to associate with small-town living or with powerful clans such as the Kennedys. Furthermore, since Spaniards typically start dating their future spouses in high school or, at the latest, university and marry in their mid or late twenties, there is a long period of courtship during which each of the partners becomes almost as closely integrated into the spouse's family—the *familia política* or in-laws—as into his or her own. The result is a dual support system, the significance of which is captured in a wry Spanish proverb: *Vive de tus padres hasta que puedas vivir de tus hijos* (Live off your parents until you can live off your children). To an outsider, it may seem that this is really what Spaniards do. If one's parents have money, it is as good as having it oneself. Americans too can expect to inherit from their parents, but in most cases they do not consider their future inheritance as affecting the amount of money they can and should earn today. However, many Spaniards generally have routine access to family money. Even these days, when the economic euphoria of the 1960s is only a memory, parents will often buy an apartment to give to their son or daughter on their wedding day. Young people will say "I have an apartment at the seaside" or "I have a cottage in the country" when in fact the property is owned by the parents. It belongs to the family and, therefore, to each member.

Family support extends into professional as well as personal life. As noted earlier, many people work in family businesses, and even in the wider work environment family ties still count. People will try to help other members of their extended family find employment in the company where they work or another company where they have influence. The central importance of personal contacts, which will be discussed in more detail later, starts with the family. Relatives and in-laws routinely help out younger members of the family; this tradition is becoming, if anything, stronger as high levels of unemployment in Spain persist and work is difficult to find.

Given these circumstances, the foreigner should not be surprised to find that a Spanish colleague's professional network includes many family members and reaches out into the extended family to include cousins, godparents and in-laws. While the average Spanish employee does not have a photograph of spouse and children on his or her desk, family members probably impinge more on working life than the smiling figures pictured on the American's desk.

Most national *convenios* or job agreements give employees the right to days off for family emergencies such as severe illness or death of a family member. There is a short period (several days) of paternity leave for men whose wives have just had a baby, while a three-month paid maternity leave, still a dream in the U.S., is the legal norm in Spain. A Spaniard who goes into the hospital can expect to have family there for every minute of visiting hours. Private clinics, which allow visitors round the clock, even provide beds for family members in the patient's room, since someone will be there for every hour of the day and night. Female employees with children under school age are entitled to leave work an hour earlier each day. And most husbands will take time off work to accompany their pregnant wives on routine visits to the doctor.

The link between the family network and professional life in Spain is something many Americans vaguely disapprove of. It seems to smack of nepotism and other concepts alien to the American ideal of self-reliance and independence. Naturally, there are cases of incompetents who have obtained, through enchufe, positions they do not deserve. However, in most cases the existence of connections creates a relationship of loyalty and obligation that can enhance an employee's value.

Spaniards, for their part, generally have mixed feelings about American family style. They think desktop photographs of family are cute but odd. As for the American habit of taking off to the other side of the country or the world without a backward glance, most Spaniards are both envious and dismayed. They can see the benefits of not having to deal with the relationships involved in a close family network, but they can also see the disadvantages of doing without the support the family network provides. Most Spaniards would probably say, "It's all right for them, but it wouldn't do for me."

Americans in Spain should beware of careless talk about family. Mother-in-law jokes, for instance, are not common currency. Also, discussing personal or family matters is something Spaniards do only with intimates. Workmates may fall into this category, since many Spaniards work so long in the same company that their workmates become another "family," but the American, who is by definition a temporary visitor, should hesitate before discussing family or personal matters, especially problems. In Spain, as in most European countries, people are far more reserved in this respect than Americans and feel uncomfortable when personal information is thrust upon them.

Groups and Communities

Class

Egalitarianism is one of the most cherished American ideals. Many Americans will affirm that the U.S. is a classless society, while Europe is straitjacketed by class consciousness. The "rags to riches" ideal of a person who can start off as nobody and rise to wealth and power, as many have done in the U.S., is difficult to imagine in Europe. The influence in the U.S. of European immigrants in search of a better life and more opportunity has contributed to a belief among many Americans that social systems in Europe are unjust and even feudal. It sometimes seems that Americans who come to Spain are looking for confirmation of this belief and are predisposed to find signs of rigid class structures. They latch on gleefully to the idea of enchufe, for instance, as proof that in Spain, unlike the U.S., "It's not what you know, but who you know." At the same time many U.S. companies trying to establish themselves in Spain want to make use of upper-class networks of money and influence and set out to recruit at least some of their top executives from socially prominent families. This may lead to a kind of confused schizophrenia in top American managers based in Spain, who find themselves playing a game they not only may disapprove of but also do not fully understand.

In Spain, social classes are clearly defined and are strongly influenced by historical developments. During the reconquest of Spain from the Muslims, the society underwent a process of social reorganization and re-Christianization. Social status came from being an "old Christian," not a convert. It also meant being pure-blooded, without Moorish or Jewish ancestry. In many parts of Spain a gentleman, in addition to being an old Christian with pure blood, was also someone who had never worked for his living, but who fought in the reconquest and was rewarded with lands off which he then lived. To be upper class in Spain in those days meant a life of idleness and attitudes of religious intolerance and racial exclusiveness. This is a far cry from the American ideal of Horatio Alger, in which status is achieved through hard work, the result of which is the accumulation of money and social influence.

What residue of the fifteenth century still remains in Spanish society? Much and little. Everyone in Spain is officially Catholic, though in fact there are synagogues, mosques and a constellation of Protestant churches; and the percentage of the population that goes to church regularly is smaller in Spain than in the U.S. (a fact which comes as a shock to many Americans). The extreme right wing of Spanish politics is fiercely Catholic and openly anti-Semitic and anti-Muslim. There are still huge estates owned by individuals and worked by tenant farmers, especially in Andalucía. The aristocracy is alive and well, and every day even

El País, an independent newspaper that is distinctly left of center, carries on its society page announcements of aristocratic titles that have been inherited, reinstated or solicited. In the phrase of one American commentator, the jet set of Madrid is "studded with dukes and playboys." However, an educated, middle-class meritocracy has been clearly on the rise for some years.

An important relic of the high status of idleness is the denigration of manual labor. "Do-it-yourself" has begun to catch on but mainly because the cost of home repairs and redecoration has risen steeply. Very few Spaniards would show the kind of pride in a manual job well done that leads Americans to display their handiwork (painting, carpentry, gardening) to visitors.

Another significant fact is that in Spain people do not do work that crosses class lines. It would be unheard of for a person from the middle class to take such jobs as delivering newspapers or waiting tables, which are part of growing up in middle-class America. Many university students work, but in teaching or white-collar jobs. Class distinctions are perpetuated through this equation of jobs to social status. In the U.S., while employment and social status are related, there is also the belief that any job is okay if you need the money. Such pragmatism is very American; a Spaniard would feel that, with family to help, you should never need the money so badly that you are willing to take a low-status job.

In Spanish corporations, the higher echelons are still filled to a great extent by the upper class. Even though there is now a rising generation of middle-class professionals, members of the moneyed upper classes have traditionally had better opportunities. At a time when English was still not widely taught in the public schools, children of the Spanish well-to-do had English tutors and were sent to summer camp in England or Ireland for the finishing touches. From private schools they moved on to private institutes for further education. At these schools they associated with their social peers and established the contacts that then led to internships in international companies, work experience in the U.S., and so on. These are the people that

American companies tend to hire, both because their qualifications are superior and because their social position ensures that they have good contacts with the world of money and influence. Top executives and, to a certain extent, executive secretaries are from the upper classes. The rude slang word for them in Spanish is *pijos*, meaning spoiled rich kids. By tradition and experience, they are often pro-American, which is another factor that makes them desirable to American companies. In dealing with them, however, an American manager may be shocked at some of the attitudes they express, especially those that betray racial, religious and class prejudices that an American would hesitate to express publicly because they go so much against the grain of the egalitarian American ideal. Furthermore, the attitudes of these people tend to vary substantially from those of the solid middle class who make up the bulk of the white-collar employees.

City and neighborhood
An American woman, recently arrived in Barcelona, was staying with her Spanish boyfriend in the area of the city that is said to equal Calcutta in population density and lack of open spaces. Low-cost high-rise apartment buildings line a road that is one of the highway accesses to Barcelona, with all the attendant noise and pollution. After a few days, the woman said, "I want to see where the rich people live." Accordingly, her friend took her to the "upper zone," as it is called. The streets were quieter and the apartment buildings were handsome and surrounded by small patches of lawn or shrubbery. There was usually a *portero* or doorman who monitored visitors and kept everything in order. "But," said the American despairingly, "they're still apartments."

Indeed, Spanish city dwellers live in apartments. Many own a chalet in the countryside or an apartment at the beach to which they retire for weekends and vacations. But suburbs, with separate homes standing in their own yards, are restricted to a few modern developments (*urbanizaciónes*) around the big cities. Because of this great physical difference between Spanish

American cities, Americans often have a hard time perceiving that Spanish cities also have neighborhoods. That is to say, each city has not only its old and new areas, its rich, middle-income and decayed zones—as do most North American and European cities—but also specific and very clearly defined neighborhoods, not more than a few blocks square, that are little communities with stable populations. They are in fact like villages within the city, and it is common for people to live all their lives in one such village. Of course, this is not true of everyone. Some people move from one part of the city to another to be nearer their work or their families, and a few move out of the city to an urbanización. Huge old apartments in the city centers are now being bought and restored by well-to-do professionals. Nonetheless, the majority of people think of themselves as living in a particular neighborhood.

The idea of neighborhoods in Spanish cities is particularly surprising to Americans because Spaniards do not seem to be neighborly in the American sense. People do not go to one another's homes, but rather meet in the local café. It is most unusual for neighbors to drop in on one another except to discuss a mutual problem, such as a leaky pipe. Further, apartment dwelling in large American cities tends to be impersonal, and those living in apartments know little or nothing about the people living around them. Because of these factors, Americans living in Spain don't think of themselves as having (or being) neighbors. But the Spanish do regard one another as such. In fact they probably know everything there is to know about one another, especially if there is a portero or portera, whose main, though not official, function is to keep tabs on everyone and pass on gossip. One can be sure that the arrival of anyone new is noted and commented upon, especially when that new person is a foreigner.

Americans living in a Spanish apartment building should accordingly make a point of greeting people they meet in the elevator or in the lobby or when shopping at local stores and markets (which they should do even though driving halfway across the city to a big "hypermarket" may be more familiar and easier to deal with). Becoming part of the neighborhood will help Americans more quickly feel at home.

Spanish ID cards and many official forms carry the phrase *natural de...*(native of...), which refers to the city, town or village of one's birth. Most Spaniards are still living in their hometowns, though there are people who have moved from one part of the country to another for professional or economic reasons. In particular, people from small towns or villages moved into the big cities in large numbers in the 1950s and early 1960s. However, mobility is far less common than in the U.S. The propensity of Americans for moving from one place to another is a source of wonder to many Spaniards. What particularly strikes Spaniards is that when an American is asked where he or she is from, the answer is the name of the current place of residence. For example, an American says, "Well, I'm from Minneapolis, though I was born in Chicago." A Spaniard, on the other hand, will answer, "I'm from Zaragoza, though I've been living in Madrid for twenty-five years," because of a much stronger sense of identification with his or her native city.

Much is said about the traditional rivalry between Madrid (capital of Spain) and Barcelona (capital of Catalonia), and it does exist, but it is not peculiar to these two cities. Spaniards tend to identify strongly with their hometowns, and the rivalry and competition between different cities surprises many Americans. Regional identity is often an undercurrent in debates about the virtues and shortcomings of different cities. The issue of Catalan nationalism is an important factor in the Madrid-Barcelona rivalry. This type of competition is something that Americans usually find hard to take seriously, but they can make it work to their advantage. Spaniards, being proud of their cities, are always happy to show them off or to advise newcomers on places to go or things to see. By getting to know the city, Americans will feel more at home themselves and will also win the goodwill of Spanish acquaintances, thus easing the process of settling in.

Attitudes toward Authority

Self-discipline

The concept of self-discipline is one of the biggest stumbling blocks to successful interaction between Spaniards and Americans, since it is one of the areas of greatest difference. Americans, either because of the Puritan tradition or a pragmatic sense of its usefulness, value self-discipline.

One way self-discipline is instilled in people is through childhood training, and in this respect there is a great difference between Americans and Spaniards. While some cultures (British, French and German, for example) see Americans as too permissive with their children, Spaniards indulge theirs far more. Americans are amazed, for instance, to see children out and about with their parents at midnight and shake their heads disapprovingly about the fact that children are allowed to have their own way, with parents putting up only a nominal resistance.

Serious trouble can be encountered in American-Spanish marriages when it comes to raising children. The American is invariably stricter than the Spanish spouse and much more so than the Spanish in-laws. Americans sometimes attribute the lack of self-discipline among Spaniards to overindulgence as children. Spaniards appear to be taught from earliest childhood that rules can always be bent if one wants something badly enough. Since Spanish parents don't seem to draw a clear line between what one wants and what one can have, their children, in the American view, do not learn the difference between what they want and what is good for them, which is the basis of self-discipline.

Furthermore, self-discipline comes to some extent from a sense of the needs of others, and Spaniards are notoriously indifferent to such needs. Despite the strong sense of community, Spaniards describe themselves as *insolidarios* (lacking in solidarity). To counter this, the city council of Madrid at one point adopted the slogan *Vivimos en comunidad* (We're a community) as part of a consciousness-raising campaign concerned

32

with social problems. The idea of good citizenship, which in Spanish is called *civismo*, is something that most Spaniards associate wistfully with other countries. Many trivial irritations experienced by Americans living in Spain derive from this lack of civismo and inability to attribute importance to the needs or rights of others.

Littering is one example. The streets and sidewalks of Spanish cities are strewn with scraps of paper and cigarette butts. It is safe to say that a Spaniard's first instinct in disposing of an unwanted item is to throw it on the ground. One American mother in Spain told of buying a cupcake for her child in a bakery. There was no wastebasket visible, so the mother told the child to put the paper wrapper on the counter. The woman behind the counter good-naturedly scolded the child for putting rubbish on the counter. "Throw it on the floor!" she said. In Spanish cafés and bars, all the wastepaper and crumbs from the counter are routinely swept onto the floor, creating a mess that is not cleaned up until closing time and that has dissuaded more than one foreigner from venturing in.

Fernando Diaz-Plaja, in *The Spaniard and the Seven Deadly Sins*,[2] graphically describes the way Spaniards arriving late for a movie will make a noise, talk loudly to one another and generally act oblivious to the fact that they are disturbing other, more punctual moviegoers who are trying to watch the film. American teachers in Spain have found that at exam time students who hand in their papers and leave the room early almost always stand just outside discussing the test in loud voices, without taking into consideration that they might be impeding the concentration of those still taking the exam.

The majority of bars, discotheques and restaurants in Spain are in regular storefront premises, with several floors of apartments above. Most of these places of entertainment have a rather pathetic sign on the front door saying *Respeten el descanso de los vecinos* (Please respect the sleep of our neighbors), in the hope of discouraging people who leave in the small hours of the morning from whooping it up, which of course the departing patrons do anyway.

The mistake that Americans often make is to think that inconsiderate behavior is deliberate or malicious in intent. Nothing could be further from the truth. In all these instances, if asked to stop making the noise, Spaniards will invariably apologize and do their best to keep their voices down. The initial irritant, however, is there: Spaniards do not think about other people until the fact that they are annoying them is called to their attention. What happens most commonly is that Americans, expecting Spaniards to be more considerate, assume that by being noisy or otherwise *insolidarios*, Spaniards are deliberately trying to be offensive. The typical response of Americans is to suffer in resentful silence, suppressing their feelings until things become intolerable, and then to react angrily. Spaniards are usually amazed by the vehemence with which Americans vent their feelings and say soothingly, *Haberlo dicho, hombre* ("Why didn't you say something before?"). This usually does not mollify Americans, because what they are really objecting to is not so much the behavior as the attitudes behind it. If they are sufficiently irritated to start criticizing the manners of the Spaniards, then real trouble is likely to follow, since any accusation of having bad manners or being boorish (*maleducado*) is an insult in Spain. Unfortunately, *maleducado* is frequently the word Americans choose to describe someone who is simply being undisciplined in the American sense.

The individual and the law

Americans believe in a government of, for, and by the people. Laws, as expressions of popular will, can be modified as the people wish, and incompetent officials can be held accountable. Further, Americans believe, in the efficiency of government. Above all, they believe in the right and responsibility of individuals to participate in their government.

All of this produces a largely law-abiding population, but one whose members are ready to engage in direct political action. If a law seems unreasonable, Americans feel they have a right, and even a duty, to change it; but they abide by it while it stands. Here, again, is a deep gulf between Americans and Spaniards.

In the Spanish colonies in the Americas, there was a phrase often used by the servants of the Spanish crown: *Obedezco, pero no cumplo* (I obey but do not comply). Regulations that were seen as inappropriate were not questioned, but somehow they were conveniently ignored or circumvented. There was a good reason for this attitude: the colonies were run from Spain, and it often took years for messages to be sent and decisions to be made and communicated. Meanwhile, everyday government had to go on in the colonies, and go on it did, without too much concern for the letter of the law.

This bit of history serves as a metaphor for current Spanish attitudes toward the law and toward external authority in general. Spain is inordinately bureaucratic, and the ordinary citizen responds by trying to get around the system. There is a proverb, *Hecha la ley, hecha la trampa*, which means "Every law has its loophole." This is the way things appear to work in Spain, much to the discomfort of Americans. The advent of computers is bringing change, but slowly. Until recently, for instance, Spaniards have been quite contemptuous of parking tickets. City dwellers collected sheaves of unpaid tickets, which they had no intention of doing anything about. Why should they? It's the city's fault if the citizens park illegally—there should be more parking places or parking garages.

Parking tickets bring out all the *pícaro* in many Spaniards. The pícaro is a Spanish folk figure who first appeared in literary form in the anonymous sixteenth-century work *La vida de Lazarillo de Tormes y de sus fortunas y adversidades*. Lazarillo de Tormes was a young boy who served a number of masters, including a blind man, an impoverished knight and a priest. The book is the tale of his adventures and misfortunes. The creed by which the boy lived was "Look out for yourself"—and he did, through thick and thin. Lazarillo was only the first of many pícaros to appear in Spanish literature, and the word *pícaro*, which can only unsatisfactorily be translated as "rascal," lives on in contemporary Spanish.

The pícaro also surfaces when Spaniards have to deal with taxes. For tax purposes, they routinely declare the value of real estate they have bought at slightly more than half the real value. Everyone knows this: the person selling, the person buying, the real estate agents, the notary, and presumably *Hacienda* (the Spanish Treasury). The thought of such blatant disregard for the law puts many Americans in a cold sweat. Even though forms of petty tax fraud, including underevaluation of property, are also practiced by Americans, they just aren't so flagrant about it. For Spaniards, declaring property at its full value is inconceivable. Recently, Hacienda has begun to tighten up on this practice; whether its efforts will be successful remains to be seen. In 1991 the Spanish *Ministerio de Economia* reported that an estimated 39 percent of Value Added Tax had not been paid.

The issue of smoking on Spanish trains also points up the complex relationship between the individual and the law in Spain. Smoking was forbidden on trains when Franco was alive, but after his death people started smoking wherever they pleased. Then Renfe (the Spanish railway company) prohibited smoking again in all carriages and put up "No Smoking" signs—but ashtrays were left in place, and people continued smoking. Later, Renfe again changed the rules and provided both smoking and nonsmoking carriages. People went on smoking wherever and whenever they wished. If someone pointed out that smoking was prohibited, they invariably said, *Es igual* ("It's all the same") and that they didn't care what the sign said. But if asked to stop smoking because it bothered other people, they would stop. This contrasts sharply with the American willingness to obey impersonal laws and regulations. Spaniards have an aversion to obeying bureaucratic rules and regulations; a personal request is more real and more important.

Another example of differing perceptions of regulations occurred in a multinational company in Barcelona. The company cafeteria, in accordance with American regulations, was dry; no alcohol was allowed. One day a major corporate deadline had been met early, and it was announced that work would end early and there would be a celebration in the cafeteria. The Spanish staff automatically went out and bought bottles of *cava* (Catalan champagne) without which no party is complete. For the Spaniards, the no-alcohol rule was one thing, but cava at a party was another. However, when the American managers arrived, they saw only a breach of company rules and ordered the offending bottles removed.

Another example of the difference between Spanish and American attitudes in regard to rules and regulations is exam-taking behavior. Americans who teach Spaniards learn that at exam time Spaniards will invariably look at one another's papers unless the seating arrangements in the room actively prevent it. Everyone does this—the best-prepared students as well as the worst prepared. Even the terminology of this behavior is significantly different: Spaniards call it *copying*, a far more neutral term than the American word, *cheating*, which carries a strong connotation of moral disapproval. Many an American teacher has been reduced to helpless fury by the sight of students sitting side by side, blatantly looking at one another's exam papers. Americans see this behavior as dishonorable; Spaniards merely see it as practical: "Everyone copies in exams, and if you don't want us to, you should separate the chairs."

Spanish students are used to a system in which, among other things, they may be examined on material not taught during the course. Exams are often arbitrary, unfair, skewed or designed to make a certain number of students fail. Given this, copying becomes a logical form of self-protection. Two Americans taking an M.B.A. in Barcelona said that one of the things they learned was to copy in exams. The work load was excessive, the content of exams was unpredictable and arbitrary; and when the choice was to fail (unfairly) or to copy, they copied. They didn't cheat, which implies dishonest use of a fair system. Rather, they copied, which implies necessary self-protection from an unfair system.

To understand this behavior one must return again to the

colonial mind-set of *obedezco, pero no cumplo*. What the colonial period had in common with the present, or at least the recent past, was the arbitrariness of laws and regulations, in the face of which the individual was impotent. Authority was often equivalent to repression, and the only way left open to the individual was that of the pícaro. One of the hardest tasks for the government of Spain during the years since the restoration of democracy has been to rebuild the individual's confidence that government is made up of human beings who are accountable, of laws that can be modified or thrown out, and of institutions that are there to serve the people and not vice versa. In 1987 the city council of Barcelona initiated a program called *Faci d'Alcalde* (You Be the Mayor). Its purpose was to allow individuals who had ideas for the improvement of their neighborhoods to present them to the city council, along with plans for their execution, budgets, etc. There was some response, but it was disappointing from such a large city with so many problems.

A change in Spanish mentality regarding government and the law will not occur overnight. Spaniards still have to be convinced of what Americans believe implicitly: that the system can be fought. When Americans in Spain stand up for their rights, their Spanish friends often try to dissuade them, saying: "You're just a private individual. You can't change the system." If Americans do effect change, Spaniards react with amazement and perhaps with a sneaking suspicion that being American helped.

These attitudes toward law and authority constitute a profound difference between Spaniards and Americans. The Americans who have come to terms with this difference are those who understand the mentality and its origins and recognize that the "American way" cannot automatically be transplanted to another society with a different history and different traditions. They also realize that Spanish society is remaking itself and that there are still many contradictions and inconsistencies.

Confianza: *Trust in Spanish society*
The arrival of warm spring weather in Spanish cities brings with it several characteristic sights: the swallows that nest in the eaves of buildings and swoop through the air at early morning and dusk; the outdoor café tables where people sit and eat or drink at all hours; the tour buses with flocks of tourists being shepherded to the sights; and then the long lines of these same tourists, reporting to their respective consulates or embassies that their wallets have been stolen or their purses snatched. To the angry tourist who has lost passport, money, tickets and traveler's checks and has had a vacation ruined, Spain is a dangerous place. Levels of both unemployment and drug addiction are high in Spanish cities, and petty crime, especially street crime, has increased enormously in recent years. The tourist, of course, is easy prey anywhere. Residents blend in, both in appearance and in behavior, and know where not to go and how to spot trouble coming, though they too can be the victims of theft or other crime in Spain.

What is striking, however, is that most Americans living in Spain tend to comment not so much on the incidence of crime as on the extent to which Spanish society seems to run on *confianza*. Confianza means not confidence but trust. *Una persona de confianza* is a person who can be trusted. Perhaps the longevity and stability of work relationships and the fact that so many Spaniards are living and working in the town where they and their families have always lived contributes to the importance of confianza. In a stable environment, reputation is very important. It is possible that Americans who move to Spain are already so far away from their hometowns that they have lost touch with this kind of relationship, which is by no means unique to Spain.

In the U.S., as elsewhere, the corner store where you buy a paper every day is more likely to let you owe a dollar than the department store where you are just one of thousands of customers per week. Spain is no different in this regard. However, what surprises Americans is how quickly they can obtain people's trust, even when a considerable amount of money is involved.

In one instance, an American resident in Barcelona had to make three plane reservations from Barcelona to Germany for family members. The cost was substantial and the American could only get a part of it out of the bank in one day with his cash card, yet the tickets had to be issued and paid for that day. His solution was to ask some fellow Americans at his office to lend him the money until the next day, when he could withdraw more from the bank. Overhearing him, one of his Spanish colleagues said, "Do they know you at the travel agency?"

"Well, I've been there before."

"Then there shouldn't be any problem. Ask the travel agency if you can give them what you have as a deposit and then pay the difference tomorrow. They're bound to say yes if they know you."

Sure enough, the travel agency issued the plane tickets without full payment.

Spain abounds with this type of anecdote. Either a store has a sign prominently displayed, saying "We do not take checks," or else checks are accepted, often without even adding the check writer's name, address and phone number on the back. Every neighborhood grocery store has a notebook with the names of people who maintain accounts at the store and very often shop without money. *Ya me lo pagará mañana* (You can pay me tomorrow) is a common phrase.

Americans often find Spanish confianza very pleasant, but it can also make them uncomfortable because they are not accustomed to this style of dealing with people. An American trained in a U.S. corporate culture may balk, for instance, at Spanish interviewing and hiring procedures, which tend to rely much more on whether the person and his or her family are known and are de confianza than on the details of education and professional background, the appearance of the résumé and the number and quality of letters of recommendation. Similarly, an American entering into contract negotiations may be disconcerted at the amount of information that is taken for granted or left unclear. Spaniards often feel there is no need to pore over details, since everything can be worked out satisfactorily as long as the person one is dealing with is de confianza.

To Americans, this reliance on confianza is often perceived as being inefficient. The person who is de confianza may be wrong for the job. Negotiations frequently leave the way open for later confusion, misunderstandings and mistakes because verbal agreements based on confianza rather than hard bargaining carefully translated into written contracts have been forgotten or misremembered.

Americans living in Spain must walk a fine line here. On the one hand, Spaniards admire American efficiency and detail consciousness. On the other hand, the American who persists in imposing the American style, who demands too many letters of recommendation or insists on every detail in writing, may appear overly suspicious and lacking in trust. The other side of giving trust is that one also expects to receive it; Spaniards who know themselves to be de confianza will be offended by suspicion.

Americans often do not really trust Spaniards to attend to detail and to remember everything that has been said or to judge accurately a person's abilities or qualifications when there is not much written evidence to back them up. However, if the American is not careful, the Spaniards will perceive this mistrust in a much more global sense, as an imputation that they are basically untrustworthy people, which in most cases is not the intention of the American. But serious trouble can result when Spaniards feel their character has been impugned. The best thing Americans can do in these situations is to slacken their pace, pin down as much detail as possible without communicating mistrust, and then back off. What is not worked out to the last detail in one meeting can be worked out in the next or the following. It is usually better to postpone something than to alienate people critical to your operation. It is also helpful in these situations if Americans don't take themselves too seriously. In asking for more details, they might say something like, "You know how Americans are; we like every detail to be down on paper," thereby distancing themselves emotionally from their professional attitudes. What they are really saying, though not in so many words, is, "This is the way people in my culture do things, and even if you think it's foolish, I can't help being a foolish American, so why don't you humor me?" This will make it easier for the Spaniards, in turn, to distance themselves from their own emotional reactions and to say to one another, "Well, they're just being American; let's humor them," as opposed to "What's wrong with them? Why are they being so American?"

3

Relationships

There are dramatic contrasts between Spanish and American styles of pursuing and maintaining close relationships. The most important lies in the permanence and high degree of intimacy which characterize Spanish friendships compared to what is felt by many observers to be a tentativeness and superficiality in American friendship patterns. Sex roles and relationships between men and women also vary markedly between the two cultures and are frequent causes of misunderstanding and conflict when Spaniards and Americans encounter each other. These issues are discussed in detail in this chapter.

Friendship Patterns

Making friends
The geographic mobility typical of life in the U.S. plays a major role in determining the nature of American friendship patterns. Because Americans move from place to place and change jobs frequently, they develop the ability to establish new relationships quickly and easily. This is accomplished in a variety of ways: in school; through one's job, hobbies or club life; at parties; through church or temple; and by participating in sports. One of the reasons this process is quick and easy is that Ameri-

cans often compartmentalize their relationships into "friends from work," "friends from the team," and so on.

One American social habit that facilitates an immediate rapport with a new acquaintance is that of asking personal questions and volunteering personal information. So ingrained is this in the American style that the formation of phrases and questions about personal matters is a part of every basic course in American English for foreigners. Spaniards, like many Europeans, are made uncomfortable by this barrage of personal questions and information.

For Spaniards, making friends follows a very different pattern. Children usually spend all their school years in the same school with the same friends, and if they go to college, it is usually in their home city, and very often with at least some of their friends from school. Starting a new job is a time to make new friends for Spaniards as for Americans, but most Spaniards do not change jobs very often. For most Spanish men, the year of compulsory military service is the only time when they will associate with a wholly new group of people. As with Americans, new friends are made through one's job, hobbies or club life, but friendships tend to develop slowly, over a period of years. As for church, it is often far less of a social institution than in the U.S., and the percentage of regular churchgoers is lower in Spain than in the U.S. Finally, parties are not the same. In Spain, groups of people who already know one another go out together. If the organizer of the evening has invited people who do not know one another, the chances are that at the end of the evening they still will not know one another. Only at a second or third meeting will they begin to learn names and chat, but they are unlikely to establish a relationship independently of the person who originally brought them together. When Americans living in Spain throw parties, inviting everyone they know and expecting them to mingle, the Spanish guests typically arrive in groups which stay together for the whole evening, often causing the American hosts considerable bewilderment or frustration.

When Spaniards go on vacation, they become expansive and

friendly, easily striking up conversations and acquaintanceships with strangers. Americans can relate to this with no difficulty. However, when fall comes, the summer lifestyle disappears. Spending a summer vacation at a beach resort in Spain is no preparation for living year-round in a big Spanish city. This is a trap into which many foreigners have fallen, and many a midwinter depression has been the result.

Friendship and intimacy

Just as mobility teaches Americans to make friends frequently and quickly, it also encourages them to give up friendships with some degree of ease—an ability that has earned Americans a reputation for superficiality in personal relationships. There may be Christmas cards or occasional phone calls, but often the relationship is over once constant contact ceases.

Friends are a stable part of a Spaniard's world. It is not unusual for men who became friends in the *mili* (military service) to maintain that friendship through life. Friends may meet infrequently by American standards, yet the relationship does not suffer and is not considered to have lapsed.

Americans leaving Spain often find it much harder to say good-bye to Spanish friends than to American friends. While other Americans can easily accept that friendships change with circumstances, Spaniards are typically disconsolate at the prospect of saying good-bye to a friend because, for a Spaniard, friends are for keeps.

However, Americans are usually surprised to find that Spanish friendships can be superficial by American standards, meaning that they are lacking in intimacy, not sincerity. There is an institution, characteristic of Madrid but found all over Spain, called the *tertulia*. This is a circle of friends, typically men, who meet regularly in the same place, usually a bar or restaurant— since Spanish homes are much less open to outsiders than are American homes. The members of a tertulia are always the same. They may be of varying ages, though usually not many of them are young, since a tertulia is usually too sedate for young

46

people. There are certain dominant figures, and others who normally defer to them. The purpose of the tertulia is to sit and talk—about literature, current events, bullfighting, soccer or whatever. The most famous tertulias have included people prominent in letters or public life. The tertulia tends to be a male institution, perhaps because men have traditionally had the leisure to sit around in cafés talking, or because women have not been encouraged to do so.

What is very Spanish about the tertulia is that people can belong to one for years, seeing one another almost daily, and yet know very little about one another's personal lives. Americans are amazed at Spaniards' capacity to call someone a friend, see that person regularly over a considerable period, and still not know what the person does for a living or about many other aspects of their lives that Americans expect to know immediately. It is hard for Americans to think of such a relationship as a friendship.

Americans often find that after a period of some months in Spain, when they expect to have made some friends, all they seem to have made are acquaintances to have coffee or go out for drinks with. What Americans are looking for, in addition to pleasant social relationships, is intimacy—someone with whom to discuss fears, problems and ambitions. For Spaniards, intimate topics and problems are discussed only with family. Friends are strictly for having fun with. Friends supplement intimate family relationships rather than serving as a substitute for them. Americans in Spain lack the family support most Spaniards take for granted, and they therefore expect more intimacy in their friendships. Americans also tend to be in more of a hurry to make friends because they do not plan to be around for a lifetime and cannot afford to let friendships slowly ripen.

Many Americans in Spain look initially to other Americans for friends. Other Americans provide help and moral support through the initial period of language difficulties and culture shock. They also provide "instant friends" while the relationships with Spaniards are getting established. As friendships with

Spaniards develop, more of a balance is achieved between Spanish and American friends. However, Americans who associate only with other Americans, because it is easier and because they do not understand or accept the Spanish style of friendship, are depriving themselves of an enriching experience.

Relationships in the workplace
As we have seen, because of the patterns of social and family relationships in Spain, job mobility is low, especially at middle and lower organizational levels. There are other factors that help to maintain job stability. One is the high level of unemployment in Spain, resulting from prolonged economic difficulties which make jobs hard to find. People therefore tend to stay with the one they have. Another factor is the difficulty an organization has in getting rid of a contracted employee. Labor laws protect employees from dismissal, and firing someone involves either accumulating a complicated series of written admonitions based on documented offenses or else paying off the dismissed employee with one or two years' salary. People who do not like their jobs or who do them badly may nonetheless hang on for years, both because they cannot be dismissed and because they prefer the security of the present job to the risk involved in trying to find another.

Partly as a result of this low job mobility, an atmosphere of intimacy and unity among Spanish coworkers usually prevails. People spend many hours not only working side by side but also eating together and socializing during the long lunch breaks (at least two hours) that Spain, in the old Mediterranean tradition, continues to have. While in the past this enabled people to go home, eat and perhaps have a siesta during the lunch break, city dwellers today live too far away from work to go home. Many coworkers have lunch together every day, taking advantage of the *menú del día* (daily special) at nearby restaurants, which often have certain tables permanently reserved for the lunchtime regulars. Adding up working hours and the long lunch hours, many Spaniards spend up to ten hours a day in one another's company. It is therefore not surprising that coworkers become not only friends, in the American sense, but family, in the Spanish sense; that is, they know a great deal about one another's personal lives and have shared many personal and professional ups and downs.

This atmosphere of intimacy and trust in the workplace is important to Spaniards, and it directly affects their reactions to the expectations and practices Americans bring there. For instance, Americans are usually task oriented. They feel that they have come to do a job and tend to concentrate on it rather than on cultivating relationships with coworkers. What they fail to realize is that these relationships will powerfully influence their ability to get the job done. Americans who neglect to establish good relationships at work may find an absence of cooperation that eventually undermines their effectiveness. This is a dilemma because the American task-orientation and "Let's get this show on the road" attitude is also something Spaniards admire. However, it is one thing to admire an attribute that leads to greater efficiency and productivity and another to work every day with a person who is insensitive to good relations in the office. Spaniards may like what Americans accomplish without liking how they act, especially if they are poor at integrating into the familia.

Why do Americans act as they do? It may be partly because, even though they normally make friendships easily, they feel their time in Spain is going to be so short that it is not worth the effort to develop good relations. Also, Americans are often brought in to show, to teach, to manage and/or to lead. The implied message, especially in the thinking of the head office, is that no Spaniard could do the job as well. Conscious of this, Americans may feel that they are under hostile observation. It is often said that envidia (jealousy, envy) is "the Spanish vice" (el vicio español) and that Spaniards prefer to backbite and criticize rather than to openly compete. But in a work environment where people cannot be fired, open confrontation with coworkers may lead to feuding rather than clearing the air;

therefore, people keep resentments to themselves. Also, how can Spaniards openly compete with imported Americans who are also superiors in the hierarchy? Rather, they will observe the Americans, take their measure and then treat them accordingly—with trust or suspicion, openness or reserve—depending on the atmosphere the American has created. One Spanish employee of an American multinational corporation said, *Aquí hay blancos, negritos, y negritos con cualificaciones.* ("In this company there are white folks, darkies, and darkies with qualifications.") It may seem that way to many Spaniards, and whether it proves to be true or not will be influenced by the attitude of the current *blanco.*

Americans, meanwhile, may be wary of integrating, and if this wariness is interpreted as standoffishness, the imagined hostility may become real. First, the feeling of having to "show their stuff" may bring out the competitiveness in Americans. They may see the Spanish staff as rivals, even if they are subordinates, and there will probably be an element of truth in this. Those Spaniards who are qualified and motivated probably do look forward to the day when they can be in the Americans' shoes. However, in the Spanish work environment competitiveness is seen as negative whenever it interferes with good working relationships. People are not expected to compete openly for preference or advancement. Therefore, Americans who are trying to dazzle their Spanish colleagues may only be impressing them with how unpleasant they are.

Second, the Americans' loyalties and networks are still with the parent company, rather than with the local branch or office. Americans will eventually go home, and they cannot afford to let their contacts cool or to get out of touch with events and trends back home. Nonetheless, if they want to succeed in Spain, Americans must be committed and loyal to the local office. Only in this way will they get commitment and loyalty in return.

One last word about work relationships: despite the *familia* environment, work life and home life are not usually mixed.

This separation of home and work can be difficult for newly arrived Americans, who need people to socialize with. In the U.S. coworkers would be a primary source of new social relationships, but this is not the case in Spain. Most Americans begin by socializing with other Americans, then gradually build up networks of Spanish friends.

Sex Roles

Latin Lovers

On arriving in Spain, the American soon observes—or experiences—the *piropo*, a jolting reminder that this is a very different culture. The dictionary discreetly defines piropo as "a compliment" or "flattery," but that definition falls far short of describing what happens. Before the astonished and disapproving gaze of the American, a man, standing or walking along the street, calls out a remark to a passing woman (a stranger). American men find this reminiscent of low-class behavior in the U.S. American women find it galling. The piropo, also found in other southern European cultures, is usually the American woman's first experience of the Latin Lover syndrome in Spain.

The Latin Lover is now something of a joke in Spain. Pronounced with a caricature of a Spanish accent—*Lateen Loberr*—it brings to mind the era when Spain first became the summer playground of Europe. At that time northern European and American women who came to Spanish beach resorts in the summer represented societies where women were far more liberated than in Spain. A myth sprang up around *suecas* (Swedes) which became the umbrella term for all blonde foreign women. Because of the free-and-easy holiday mood and the greater degree of sexual freedom of their cultures, suecas were equated with loose morals. Men who worked in hotels, restaurants and discotheques at the beach resorts were reputed to have their pick of sex-mad foreign females. This myth did nothing to make life easier for foreign women who visited Spain to study, see the sights or make friends.

The origins of the Latin Lover myth probably go back as far as the play *Don Juan Tenorio* by Jose Zorrilla (1817-1893). Don Juan (based on a real person) and his seductive prowess caught the imagination of Europe and has since appeared in countless forms. Spain does not have a monopoly on the Latin Lover. However, males in Spanish society have traditionally been prized from birth, pampered during childhood and adolescence and, in adult life, privileged with more personal freedom, social authority and economic power than women. *Machismo* is the cult of the male and male sexist behavior. However, Don Juan is as much the object of satire as he is of admiration in today's Spain. Els Joglars, a Catalan theater group famous in Spain for its savagely irreverent plays, portrayed in *Els Virtuosos de Fontainebleau* an encounter between a Frenchwoman and a bullfighter's cloak, symbol of male daring and virility. To her disgust, she found the symbol to be more than the reality.

Don Juan may be only an old story and the Latin Lover an overplayed myth, but there is no doubt that the differences between Spanish and American sex roles and relationships can create problems in male-female interactions.

Americans tend to enter romantic relationships and marriage on their own, without depending on their families for support and sometimes even without family involvement. If problems arise, the couple may seek help from professional counselors; if the problems persist, the marriage is dissolved. Spaniards, like many foreigners, are struck by the speed with which some American couples move from the wedding reception to the divorce court. This pattern of relationships reflects certain values and attitudes shared by most Americans: the assumption that an individual is responsible for his or her own life, the idealistic belief that somehow one can (or should) make one's own life situation perfect, and a certain intolerance for ambiguous or contradictory circumstances.

In Spain, male-female relationships have traditionally been influenced by the definition—common in Latin countries—of woman's role as either mother or mistress. Until a generation ago, Spanish women were expected to be very conscious of personal appearance only until marriage. Once they were married and particularly once children arrived, women were expected to embrace the mother role completely. It was faintly improper for a married Spanish woman to watch her weight or to dress in youthful fashions. Meanwhile, many husbands found other women to play the mistress role. Wives often knew of these liaisons but could do nothing about them, principally because divorce was unobtainable. Support from the extended family and her social status as a married woman helped many a Spanish woman to live with a situation that would have driven her American counterpart to the divorce court.

While the legalization of divorce in Spain has given both men and women an escape from unacceptable marital situations, the definition of *unacceptable* is probably not as narrow as it is in the U.S. In particular, Spaniards are more cynical than Americans about extramarital affairs. The 1987 withdrawal of Gary Hart from the race for the Democratic presidential nomination because of the scandal caused by newspaper reports of his extramarital adventures mystified most Spaniards, unless they realized that the issue was not only of Hart's sexual behavior but also his stability, integrity and ability to deal with crises. An American male teacher married to a Spanish woman was surprised to find that his female students, knowing he was married, nonetheless flirted with him. For the American, flirting with a married man was the first step to what could be serious involvement and the termination of his marriage. For the students, flirting was an amusement that probably would not lead to serious involvement and even if it did would not affect the marriage.

Single American women complain of the lack of a singles scene in Spain, which is explained in part by the fact that many couples still stay together for the sake of the family or the children. In other words, the number of divorced people at loose ends is much smaller in Spain than in the U.S. Many American women find they are expected to play the role of mistress, or else go out with far younger men who are not yet married. It is a hard choice: loneliness or a relationship Americans find unequal or dishonest.

As for American single men in Spain, some have also found the mistress-mother divide still firmly in place. One man entered what he believed to be an easy, freewheeling affair with a Spanish woman and was shocked when she announced she was pregnant and expected him to marry her. American men looking to get married have traditionally had no problem in Spain. Those looking for no-strings-attached relationships do better nowadays with divorced women, who are most likely to have outgrown the mistress-mother mind-set.

Change and conflict
The changes that have taken place in Spain over the last fifteen to twenty years are nowhere more evident than in relationships between the sexes. Anyone who visited Spain as recently as the early 1970s still found that female tourists were not allowed into churches if they were clad in shorts and were required to wear shawls to cover bare shoulders. In the same period, it was still *an escándalo público* (public scandal) for a couple to kiss in public, and they could be arrested for doing so. As John Hooper remarks in *The Spaniards*,[3] when one sees young women walking around on Spanish beaches nowadays, wearing only the skimpiest of bikini bottoms and nothing else, it is hard to imagine that their mothers were probably chaperoned whenever they went out in public. In 1987 a public-scandal charge brought against two women for sunbathing nude on a beach was dismissed.

These changes have come about partly because of changes in the law. In the years following the Constitution of 1978, divorce and abortion were legalized. Furthermore, contraception became more accessible, resulting in a dramatic drop in the average number of children per woman of childbearing age.

With such rapid and far-reaching changes, conflict has been inevitable. In the mid-1980s, for example, two middle-aged Spanish women of the same age and background could display radically different feelings about their children's relationships. One mother was humiliated by her son's civil marriage to a divorced woman. In her eyes a nonreligious ceremony had no validity, and she was determined not to rest until her new daughter-in-law obtained an annulment of her first marriage, thus legitimizing the second marriage in the eyes of the church. In contrast, the other mother did not turn a hair when her daughter took off for weekend camping trips with her boyfriend. "I'm sure they know what they're doing," was her only comment.

One thing that surprises foreigners who still believe Spanish society has a strict Catholic moral code is the large, vocal and sophisticated gay community in Spain, especially male homosexuals. Sitges, on the Catalan coast, is an international gay resort, and in the summer the beach is carefully demarcated into the "family" section and the "boys'" section. Similarly, Carnival in Sitges and nearby Villanova is celebrated during the day by costumed bands of children and at night by men in the wildest of drag outfits. Homosexuality is a common part of Spanish life, and this casts a different light on the outsider's concept of a society dominated by traditional males.

Contrasts such as the one between the family beach and the boys' beach in Sitges abound in modern Spain. Despite a recent swing back to the fashion of white church weddings, there are still a number of public figures in Spain who are single parents or divorcés or are living with people to whom they are not married. Though commonplace in today's world, such lifestyles are surprising in a society that also has regular vigils and processions in honor of the Virgin Mary and slogans such as *Catholics: come and honor your Holy Mother*.

Still another source of conflict, or at least tension, is the increasing number of women working outside the home. Great pressures have been brought to bear when work schedule and responsibilities conflict with, or are added to, the work and responsibilities of running a home and raising children.

Men and women at home
In the past, as in most traditional cultures, the woman took care of the home, the children and meals, while the man went out to work. In today's world, however, a great number of Spanish women work

outside the home. As a result, men's and women's roles are in transition, as they are in other countries. In some families, men continue to regard home and childrearing as the exclusive preserve of the woman. This produces the "Superwoman," who combines full-time employment with her other jobs as mother and home-maker. Other couples reach a more equitable arrangement, with both man and woman sharing joint responsibilities to a much greater extent. Sometimes within a single family married siblings may have different household arrangements, with one brother being a typical *machista* (male chauvinist) and refusing to lift a finger in the home, while another does some of the cooking and shopping or his share of taking care of the baby. In this respect there is probably as much variety of male and female roles in Spain as in the U.S., making any generalizations impossible.

Regardless of whose responsibility it is, Spaniards are proud of their homes and want them to be nicely decorated and well kept. Americans, seeing the often dingy exteriors of Spanish apartment buildings, are usually surprised to see how house-proud Spaniards are and how picture-perfect their apartments can be.

Spanish perceptions of the American home are influenced by what they see on television shows. Many Spaniards think that a proper home, with regular meals and family life, can no longer be found in the U.S. Spaniards often think of the American woman as being completely cut off from the traditional role of the home-maker—as someone who cannot cook and who farms out all the work of the household to employees. These Spaniards would be amazed to find out how many American women still bake cookies and drive the kids to Little League. Such women are not the stuff of internationally marketed television shows. Women who come to Spain on professional assignments have usually left the cook-ies-and-kiddies option far behind, and they can be critical and unsympathetic about what they see as the enslavement of Span-ish women who are juggling home, family and work. If, in addi-tion, these American women cannot cook and do not "run a nice home," they serve as confirmation of the Spanish theory of the deterioration of home life in the U.S.

Both the U.S. and Spanish societies are dealing with the same problem: conflict between the traditional structure in the home and the new realities of two-career couples. It will be easier for Americans to accept that the situation in Spain is not so different from that in the U.S. if they can manage to see the underlying similarities beneath the surface differences of machista style.

Men and women at work
Given the rapid changes that have taken place in Spain, there are inconsistencies in the Spanish workplace just as there are in the Spanish home. On the one hand, there are women mayors, presidents of companies and high-ranking government officials. On the other hand, many Spanish companies still do not give equal pay for equal work. This is absolutely contrary to the constitutional rights of women in Spain, but, as is the case in the U.S., there is a gap between the law and its application; and the process for taking a case to court is long, complicated and expensive. Many underpaid women prefer to keep quiet and not rock the boat.

Some aspects of the Spanish working scene shock Americans. Advertisements for employees may specify the gender of applicants without fear of legal repercussions. Americans are accustomed by now to equal opportunity, affirmative action and the prohibition against asking for certain kinds of personal data on job applications and résumés. American women are irritated to see that a contact person in an organization is identified as Señor González (if a man) but as Señorita Rosa (if a woman); that is, using the man's surname but the woman's first name. Most Spanish men addressing a woman for the first time will ask *¿Señora o señorita?* As in other countries, this careful distinction between married and unmarried women is gradually disappearing, but the question is still common. The only consolation for American women is that Spanish women are just as irritated by it.

Americans working in Spanish offices may be surprised at the familiarity between coworkers of opposite sexes. New clothes and haircuts are the subject of detailed comment and analysis. Women are constantly receiving piropos, which are sometimes reciprocated. In general, Americans may find that the atmosphere is not as androgynous as they would expect back home. However, even if the atmosphere does seem looser than in the U.S., Americans must remember that the Spanish coworkers are familia and their relationships are based on the trust of long acquaintanceship. It should also be noted that sexual harassment, long present in the Spanish workplace, is now becoming an issue for public debate and legislation.

4

Language and Communication

Learning Spanish

It is important that Americans going to Spain know something of Castilian. Any American who doubts this need only think about the plight of a foreigner who arrives in the U.S. unable to speak English. Even though some of their Spanish colleagues will speak English, both Spaniards and Americans in Spain agree that Americans who are unable to communicate in Castilian are at a great disadvantage. Some of the kinds of cross-cultural misunderstandings which we have noted in this book can be exacerbated to the point of conflict if there is also a serious language barrier. Furthermore, it is generally agreed that a one-month crash course in beginner's or tourist Castilian, though better than nothing, is insufficient. But Americans who can reach an intermediate level of language proficiency will be able to cope satisfactorily from their first day in Spain and to learn from what is going on around them. One of the most popular myths about language learning is that the best way to learn a language is to "just go to the country and immerse yourself in it." People who have tried this approach without prior knowledge of the language agree that they condemned themselves to feeling totally incompetent for a full year. Most

59

Americans arriving in Spain for professional reasons do not have the luxury of sounding like a fool, even for a week. Since instruction in Castilian is easily accessible in the U.S., it is difficult to understand why corporations still send their high-ranking officials to Spain without equipping them with the language.

Obviously, corporate goals cannot always wait on language classes, and the individual with the necessary know-how for an assignment in Spain may not be the one with the best knowledge of Castilian. Nonetheless, it would probably be better in the long run for the achievement of the company's purposes and for the well-being of the person being sent to Spain if departure were postponed for three months of intensive language training, as is common practice among Spanish executives, students or other visitors going to the U.S.

It is important, as well, for Americans to continue studying Castilian once in Spain, since regular classes will help them make sense of the language that is bombarding them from all sides. It can also be a good public relations move, as will be discussed later.

One comfort for Americans studying Castilian is that Spaniards are typically tolerant of foreigners trying to learn their language, in contrast, for example, to the French, whose ideal of linguistic perfection leads them to be quite demanding and critical of foreigners who speak it poorly. Spaniards may tease Americans about their accents, but the ribbing is good-natured. For the most part they are patient and will often gently correct and explain mistakes to help the learning process along.

With respect to the other languages of Spain, the position of Castilian-speaking Americans is quite delicate and depends on the length of their stay. As we have noted, the language issue in Spain is highly political and tied closely with the issue of regional autonomy. Many Basques and Catalans in particular think of themselves as belonging to nations that have been conquered or occupied by Spain. Their language is an outward sign of nationhood. Such strong feelings may be quite difficult for Americans to understand, but they are real and should not be taken lightly.

Speakers of the other languages do not normally expect newly arrived foreigners to know their language and assume that if a foreigner speaks anything it will be Castilian. In fact, Americans who have studied Catalan in the U.S. are usually greeted with disbelief, and the few Americans who speak only Catalan are regarded as prodigies. A foreigner who lives in Catalonia for one or two years will usually not be pressured to speak Catalan* and in other bilingual areas will not be pressured to speak Euskera or Gallego or Valencian.

Nonetheless, bilingual Spaniards very often slip into their own languages, even when there is a foreigner present who is theoretically not expected to understand. Americans often feel offended by this, thinking that they are deliberately being excluded or that criticism is being implied about their lack of knowledge of the language. It is much more likely, however, to be the result of absentmindedness. Outlawed during the Franco era, the regional languages were only used in intimate settings. People spoke only Castilian in public but used another language at home and with friends. Consequently, in an informal or intimate situation they still often switch unthinkingly into their own language, even if there are Americans present. Incidentally, it is not only Americans who are disturbed by this; it also annoys Spaniards who only speak Castilian.

Americans who settle into one of the bilingual areas of Spain for more than a year or two may find that the pressure to speak the regional language is greater. By staying longer, the foreigner is making a visible commitment to the place, and the natives tend to feel that learning the regional language is part of that commitment.

In Catalonia there is another reason for this pressure. The massive immigration of the 1960s brought people from other

---

*However, an American musician who joined an orchestra in Barcelona found that everyone spoke to him in Catalan, though they said magnanimously that he could speak to them in Castilian if he liked!

parts of Spain to Catalonia. Poverty-stricken villagers from Andalucía and Murcia received free one-way train tickets and temporary free accommodation on arrival. Many Catalans believe that the purpose of this government-subsidized migration was not only to provide a labor force for booming Catalan industries but also to break the back of the Catalan language. Today, many of the people who came to Catalonia at that time and have been living there for twenty or thirty years still do not speak a word of Catalan. Their children, who went to school in Catalonia, can probably speak it correctly, but they do not. This Catalan-resistant segment of the population is a source of great irritation to many Catalans, and it is because of them that foreigners find themselves pressured to speak Catalan once they are judged to have been around long enough to learn it.

Many Americans in Catalonia resist learning Catalan, either because they are afraid it will interfere with their learning of Castilian or because they simply do not want to put effort into learning Catalan when they will never have a chance to use it outside of Catalonia. Resisting Catalan or Euskera or Gallego will not endear Americans to the people of those regions of Spain, while learning a little of any of those languages will be very well received. Catchphrases and expressions are easy to learn and will help bridge the gap.

Nonverbal Communication

Formality and informality
Americans are more informal in communicating with one another than are members of most other cultures, including Spain. This informality, which manifests itself as "friendliness," is due to the principle of egalitarianism, which is a strong value among Americans. Outward friendliness is expected, and the absence of it may be construed as tenseness, standoffishness or hostility. Spaniards, like members of many older and more traditional societies, are much less likely to believe in equality between

people. The range of communication in Spain from formal to informal is much greater than in the U.S. and is determined by the situation, with strangers typically receiving the least "friendly" treatment. This strong contrast between Spaniards and Americans can lead to misunderstandings.

The 1980s Broadway show *Tintypes* consisted of a series of songs and vignettes from the turn of the century. Naturally, one part of the show was concerned with the arrival of immigrants from Europe. One such immigrant, a young man, asked directions in the street from an older man, a "real American." Grateful for the help, the immigrant in parting took off his cap and was surprised and pleased to find that the older man was offering to shake his hand. A comic routine followed, as the immigrant then tried to shake hands while the older man, following his earlier cue, started to take off his hat. Finally they shook hands and the immigrant, secure in this newfound confidence, went on to shake hands with other people he met. Taking off his cap was something that he had brought with him from Europe but left behind on the New York docks.

Times have changed since the beginning of the century, and in Spain times have certainly changed in recent years as far as formality is concerned. For example, the polite *usted* form of address has given way in many situations to the familiar *tú*. Clothing styles, manners and behavior all reflect a liberalization of the earlier formality. However, manners in general are still not as free and easy as in the U.S.

Friendliness and public seriousness
Spaniards who go to the U.S. are struck by the friendliness of Americans. One Catalan who moved to the U.S. complained that his face hurt from having to smile so much. The image of the U.S. projected in Spain through movies and television serials does not generally include friendliness, so whatever else Spaniards (who are used to American cops-and-robbers shows and intrigue-ridden family sagas) expect, they do not anticipate

that Americans will be personable and friendly. In fact, this characteristic is probably responsible for more 180-degree turns in the attitudes of visiting Spaniards than any other.

In Spain, in contrast, public decorum implies seriousness. Except at fiesta time, people tend to go about without smiles on their faces. Don Quixote was known as the Knight of the Sad Countenance and, in the days of the greatness of Spain's colonial empire, King Philip II set the style of sober black clothes with a plain white ruff around the neck, and an unsmiling face. Spaniards at that time were known all over Europe for their serious demeanor.

Americans, especially if they do not speak Spanish well, tend to be put off by unsmiling Spaniards. An American salesman on vacation in Spain, bothered by the sober faces he saw around him, started smiling at strangers to see what would happen and got in return reactions ranging from puzzlement to embarrassment, though he did get at least a few pleased grins.

Outward expression, however, does not necessarily reflect thoughts and feelings, particularly with Spaniards. One American who discovered this was a young woman traveling alone by air with a toddler and a baby. The baby was supposed to have a ticket although she was traveling on her mother's lap, and at the departure gate the airport officials, finding that the baby's ticket was missing, made the mother wait until they could find a representative of the airline to sort the problem out. Communication between them was by gestures, since neither side spoke the other's language. The American woman, reading only dour faces, assumed that she would be forced to miss her flight and burst into tears. The Spanish officials, upset by the sight of a weeping woman with a baby (the ultimate heart melter), redoubled their search for the airline representative, but it did not occur to them that a smile would be reassuring. Luckily an interpreter was able to tell the American what the Spaniards were saying: "Tell her not to cry; everything will be OK; we won't let the plane go without her." Finally the airline representative arrived and solved the problem, by which time the officials were goo-gooing at the baby, playing with the toddler, and helping the mother carry her luggage onto the plane.

Strangers versus people you know
The Spanish treatment of strangers is something that all foreigners, and particularly Americans, have to get used to. "Service with a smile" is an American concept. Spaniards love it when they go to the U.S., not just for the smile, but for what it implies: that strangers are entitled to the best service. This is in sharp contrast to Spain, where strangers are likely to encounter somber faces and unhelpful attitudes.

The result is that when Americans are dealing with the Spanish bureaucracy or seeking information or service from Spaniards, there may be serious misunderstandings. Americans expect courtesy and helpfulness, which Spaniards don't deliver. But Americans who react negatively simply assure themselves of even worse treatment the next time. The best response is to remain courteous and patient, which will help make the next interaction more pleasant. In Spain a stranger is no longer a stranger after the first encounter. From then on the relationship is *Ya nos conocemos* (We know each other), and treatment is different.

For many Americans, their first important interaction with the Spanish bureaucracy is in obtaining visas and residency and work permits. The process involves standing in line at many offices and obtaining documents with all sorts of stamps and seals on them, meanwhile never being sure whether everything is in order because nobody provides a comprehensive list of what is required. Frustration is guaranteed. However, time and again Americans find that the person who met them the first time with a set face, brusque answers and the most unhelpful manner possible, treats them on ensuing occasions with cooperation and helpfulness—if the Americans were polite and patient the first time around.

This pattern even extends to Spanish consulates in the U.S. An American man went to a consulate to obtain a visa for his wife and was turned away because she did not make the visa petition in person. Well trained after living in Spain for over a year, he remained calm and was polite. Two weeks later he returned to the consulate to apply for a permit to take his dog to Spain (his wife planned to go in a few days later for her visa). Not only did he get the permit for the dog, he also got the visa for his wife. Because someone at the consulate knew him, he was no longer a member of the anonymous public but a nice person with a problem.

Body language

Spanish social relationships usually involve a great deal more bodily contact than those in the U.S. The handshake is obligatory at the beginning and end of every conversation with an acquaintance. A conversation between strangers, such as in an information-giving situation (travel agency, public office etc.), may begin without a handshake, but it will usually end with one; and once the relationship is established, a handshake will begin and end every encounter. Many colleagues at work start the day by shaking hands.

Americans in Spain find themselves shaking hands more often than they do in the U.S., and it takes a while before they learn to offer their hands automatically. This difference between American and Spanish custom was experienced by a Spanish lawyer who worked for an organization with many American employees. After some weeks on the job the lawyer was asked by his American supervisor how things were going. "Not so well," was his reply. "I don't think your Americans trust me. They walk into my office, sit down, ask me whatever questions they have, and then they stand up, say thanks and leave. They never shake hands. I feel like a pariah." The lawyer was mystified when his boss laughed, until he was informed that Americans don't shake hands every time they enter or leave the office of someone they already know. After that he varied his approach, shaking hands with Spaniards and keeping his hands by his sides when visiting with Americans.

Spanish greetings also often include hugs and kisses. Men who are good friends usually greet each other with a hug, and men who are members of the same family often kiss each other on the cheek as well. Women and girls are always greeted by friends and family with a kiss on each cheek. When children or young teenagers are introduced to older people, they usually offer their cheek for a kiss. This can be surprising, especially for a young American male who is introduced to a quite grown-up-looking Spanish teenage girl and finds to his amazement that they are already "on kissing terms."

Even when closing letters the Spanish are affectionate. The normal ending when the correspondents know each other fairly well is *Un abrazo* (A hug), where an American would write "Cordially" or at most "Warm regards." With good friends, men write "Un abrazo" while women often write *Besos* (Kisses).

The question of when to shake hands, when to hug and when to kiss can be confusing to an outsider. The best procedure for Americans, for whom all this bodily contact is generally quite alien, is to take their cues from the Spaniards they meet and be ready for hugs and kisses as well as handshakes.

Americans touch friends and acquaintances less than Spaniards do, and they avoid touching strangers if at all possible. When by accident there is contact, they hastily apologize and move away. Americans in Spain have trouble in this regard. One American woman, who lived in Washington, D.C. before moving to Spain, said that within the first weeks she had bumped into more strangers (followed by the urge to punch them out) than in all her years in D.C. Other Americans have experienced the same annoyance, accompanied by feelings of embarrassment.

Spaniards moving among strangers in public are not preoccupied with keeping out of one another's way. They are thinking about themselves and not about the other people on the street. Therefore, they may quite often stop dead, change direction, or stand in a group on the sidewalk. All of these actions are likely to obstruct the free movement of others. Americans are not expecting people to do any of these things, since they assume that, like themselves, everyone at all times is concerned with keeping out of other people's way. Therefore, when someone stops dead or changes direction, the American tends to run right into that person. The American is typically much more upset about this than the Spaniard, who does not share the same taboo about touching strangers. The American feels embarrassed, frustrated and/or angry. But the Spaniard is breaking American rules, not Spanish rules. If someone stops dead in front of Spaniards or stands with a group blocking the sidewalk, Spaniards simply touch that person on the back or shoulder and the person then moves out of the way. In Spain, the way to move through a crowd is by touching people. When this happens to Americans, they feel that they are being shoved or jostled, which is such taboo behavior in the U.S. that Americans react with anger, like the woman who found herself wanting to punch people out. This seems to be one of the differences that takes longest to get used to. Americans who have been in Spain for a long time and have adapted in other ways to cultural differences still complain about Spanish crowd behavior. But at least they no longer feel the urge to hit people.

One thing that would seem too trivial to mention, if it were not so frequently noted by Americans, is the smell of garlic on Spaniards' breath. Garlic is an omnipresent condiment in Spanish cuisine. *Allioli* (garlic mayonnaise) is one of the great Catalan inventions and is extremely pungent, as are many other Spanish dishes. People may therefore smell of garlic, especially after lunch. One American woman said that it was a year before she realized that the "terrible" odor she so often smelled in Spain and which she had always associated with being unwashed or being an alcoholic was in fact the innocuous odor of garlic; and, worse, that she herself undoubtedly smelled the same, since she had joyfully taken to eating some of the most pungent of Spanish dishes. Spaniards may also smell of wine or brandy after lunch. We have no desire to perpetuate the stereotype of the wine-and-garlic-soaked, greasy Latin (most Spaniards also smell of soap and/or cologne), but Americans are perhaps the most hygiene- and odor-conscious people on earth; they can avoid becoming needlessly upset if they are aware of the normal odors they are likely to encounter in talking with Spaniards.

Communication Styles

Greetings and farewells

Spaniards are much more punctilious about greetings and fare-wells than are Americans. In addition to the handshakes, kisses and hugs normal among friends and acquaintances, Spaniards feel obligated to at least murmur a greeting whenever entering a space where there are other people. Whether it be an elevator, an office, a waiting room or a store, Spaniards always say *Hola* ("Hello") or *Buenos días/Buenas tardes* ("Good morning/Good afternoon"), getting a general murmured response. When leaving, they say *Adiós* ("Good-bye"). It takes Americans some time to learn to do this, accustomed as they are to entering and leaving places unannounced—which in Spain is considered rude behavior.

Another little quirk of Spanish greeting customs is that if they meet someone on the street, and are going to stop and have a conversation, they say *Hola*, but if they are simply going to pass each other, they say *Adiós*. While it seems a little strange to say good-bye when you first see someone, *Adiós* can also be translated as "Go with God," which makes the custom a little more comprehensible.

Conversation

The first thing that Americans usually notice about Spanish conversation is the volume. Interestingly, Spaniards who go to the U.S. also find Americans loud, but they are usually reacting to the piercing voices often found among Americans rather than the volume.

Spaniards, unquestionably, are loud. Signs in bars and restaurants in Andalucía warning *Prohibido cantar* (No singing) may seem strange until the first time one hears a group of Spaniards singing; even if unaccompanied by handclapping, it is deafening. The signs outside bars and nightclubs that read *Respeten el descanso de los vecinos* are trying to counteract the tendency of noisy groups to hang out in the street, *hablando fuerte* (talking loudly), as the Spaniards say disarmingly. Americans would call it yelling. One American who had lived in Spain for five years commented that his first ride in a train crowded with teenagers left him exhausted from the noise. Some time later, he was sitting on the same train in the same circumstances. The noise and confusion were the same, but he placidly read his book and talked to his neighbors and looked out of the window, oblivious to the racket. Similarly, Americans who have grown accustomed to Spain have learned to block out the noise in bars and restaurants and carry on their own conversations.

The second thing that Americans find different about Spanish conversation style is long-windedness. Americans often comment that it takes Spaniards a long time and a lot of words to say anything. If the American is in a hurry or feeling frustrated, this long-windedness seems like wasting time or beating around the bush. The American urge to get to the point differs greatly from the Spanish tendency to cover all possible bases and follow up on every idea. Spaniards generally admire American conciseness both in speech and in writing, but they only emulate it if they have worked for or with Americans. Most people in Spain talk more and longer about things than Americans consider necessary, but the longer they live in Spain, the more tolerant Americans become. Newcomers would be wise to try to learn to strike a balance between American conciseness and Spanish prolixity.

Avoidance of confrontation
One major difference often pointed out between Americans and Spaniards is that Americans are much more ready to engage in direct confrontation. American teachers in Spain often find that the expression of strong opinions frequently goes unchallenged. Americans tend to attribute this to passivity, backward thinking or lack of awareness on the part of the students. Similarly, American managers often find that their Spanish subordinates will not confront them directly, though the Spaniards may have strong feelings which they later express to coworkers. Silence to Americans generally means consent, because they

expect someone who disagrees with something to pipe up and say so. Spaniards, however, are quite likely, especially in a group, to keep quiet when someone says something they don't agree with. There are reasons for this: fear of repercussions if the person is a superior or suspicion if someone is not well known. For forty years Spaniards lived in a society where they could not speak their minds and were never sure to whom they were speaking. Such a situation breeds caution. Furthermore, Spaniards generally consider direct confrontation impolite. To contradict someone, especially in front of other people, is rude and may cause embarrassment which may later turn to anger and resentment. All this may seem underhanded to Americans, who like things to be up-front. Spaniards have a different style, however, and Americans should not interpret silence to mean consent. If Americans want to know what the other people present really think, they will have to ask those individuals personally and in private, and even then the response will be honest only if they are convinced that the questioners really want honesty.

Finally, when one Spaniard makes a comment that is not taken up by the others, it is possible that what is really happening is a bit of Yankee-baiting. Spaniards like to tease, and in particular Spanish men like to tease foreign women. If a Spanish man knows he can get a rise out of his American boss, coworker or teacher by making a provoking remark, he will probably make it, because he likes to see her jump. The others present remain silent rather than give importance to a teasing remark.

Speaking English
Studying English has been the rage in Spain since the mid-1970s. There are any number of small language schools offering classes in English, as well as highly successful television series and self-study courses sold in installments. English is now the primary foreign language taught in Spanish schools, and the national and regional governments have spent considerable sums on retraining teachers, equipping schools and designing new

curricula. The results are variable, but, in general, Spanish young people are learning English, and in many cases they are learning it well.

Among people over thirty the situation is more complicated. They went to school at a time when French was more commonly taught than English, so if they have learned English it has been since leaving high school, by going to a private academy or taking courses in England. Those who have been exposed to English through their professional activities may know it very well, while there may be others who at age fifty have never had a chance to learn any at all.

At any rate, there is no doubt that knowledge of English is one of the keys to professional advancement in Spain. A glance at the advertisements for professional positions in the Sunday papers will show that almost every opening requires knowledge of English. Older executives who are already established may be able to make it through the rest of their careers without English, but people under thirty-five realize that not knowing English will place serious limitations on future advancement.

This situation gives rise quite frequently to another manifestation of the pícaro: the desperate executives who show up at language schools demanding the most intensive English course available. Having managed to get a job by claiming to know English, they now need to learn some as fast as possible before getting caught. Times are tough and jobs are hard to find, but one can imagine the reaction of an American boss on finding out that a new employee has misrepresented his or her knowledge of English and that nobody in the hiring process caught it.

In a multinational corporation the top-ranking Spanish personnel will usually be fluent in English, but few Americans can speak Spanish well. Two problems may arise in this circumstance; the first is a double standard regarding language learning. The Spanish executives' jobs depend to some extent on their knowledge of English. It was a prerequisite to their being hired, and they may still be taking classes in their off-hours. Meanwhile, there may be American executives in the same organization who either cannot speak Spanish at all or who speak it badly and make no effort to improve. The significance of the double standard does not escape Spaniards who, by and large, resent it.

The second problem is that an English-only office environment interferes with the Americans' cross-cultural adaptation. If the Spaniards who work closely with Americans speak fluent American-accented English, they may often seem like pseudo-Americans. If, in addition, office systems are replicas of the U.S. home office, Americans may forget that they are operating in Spain, not back home in Ohio, and will have more difficulty dealing with the Spanish environment outside the office. Even if the American's Castilian is limited and major business still has to be done in English or through a translator, an attempt to compromise between English and Castilian in the running of the office is an investment, not only in a better office atmosphere, but in smoother adaptation to living and working in Spain.

5

Work

High-ranking Americans in multinational corporations or the Foreign Service are somewhat protected from experiencing the differences between Spaniards and Americans in the workplace. Their offices in Spain run to some extent on American home-office rules, and Spanish executives and senior staff have been selected because of their knowledge of American English, their experience in international business and in the U.S., and their familiarity with sophisticated modern business practices which, in most cases, follow the American model.

However, not every American working in Spain is with a multinational corporation or in a position of authority. Many have Spanish supervisors. A musician or dancer has artistic and financial directors; a sports coach has senior coaches or managers; a language teacher has school supervisors and/or directors; a university professor has department heads; and consultants have to deal with the organizations that hired them. These Americans encounter differences in the workplace head-on. Even those employed in multinationals or in purely American organizations such as the Foreign Service or the military come up against the work styles of Spanish staff (canteen workers, chauffeurs, cleaners, white-collar workers) who are probably "more Spanish" in their attitudes and behaviors than the English-speaking executives and counterparts they interact with most of the time.

Finally, Americans working in Spain have a life outside the office, where they encounter all the facets of Spanish society. Here is where the "differentness" will be most pronounced.

Attitudes toward Work

Work ethic

When asked about the difference between living in Spain and living in the U.S., both Americans and Spaniards are likely to mention the work ethic almost immediately. Americans who have settled in Spain generally say, "I don't have to work as hard here as I would in the U.S." Spaniards who have visited or lived in the U.S. comment on how hard everyone works. In other words, in the U.S. people "live to work," and in Spain people "work to live." In the U.S. work is central to people's lives, and they tend to devote all their energies to their jobs, at least from Monday to Friday, often working overtime or skipping lunch. Americans also talk about work a great deal, so that it infiltrates their leisure time.

For Spaniards, work is a way of earning a living. Most people put in their hours on the job but do not work extra hours except in the case of some ghastly crisis. Skipping lunch is virtually unheard-of. Once away from work they switch off completely until they walk back into the office again. This is one of the reasons Spanish friends sometimes do not know about one another's jobs, because talking about work is not a normal part of social life. If there were a severe problem at work that was causing personal difficulties, one might discuss it with family or intimate friends but rarely with acquaintances or in casual conversation.

Once again the difference between Spain and the U.S. may be a difference in values. In the U.S. working hard is valued, both because work is a highly esteemed activity and because it is a sign of ambition and wanting to better oneself, which is also valued. Further, through work one pursues achievement which, among Americans, is a significant source of identity and a measure of status. Although workaholism is sometimes seen as a problem, especially by sociologists and psychologists, the upwardly mobile professional mentality has helped to encourage it by idealizing high earnings and the image of the ambitious young professional who routinely works a sixty-hour week.

Many Americans expect people in Latin countries, Spain included, to be slow-moving and easygoing, taking siestas all the time and saying *mañana* whenever asked to do anything. The only parts of Spain that bear any relation to this image are the Canary Islands and Andalucía. The further north one goes, the more intense the work ethic becomes. The Basques and Catalans are famous in Spain for their industriousness and acquisitive instinct. Big-city professionals (with whom Americans are most likely to come into contact) work extremely hard, just like their counterparts in the U.S. Furthermore, Spaniards often have two jobs or combine work and study.

However, most Spaniards do not want to look driven. Workaholism is not fashionable in Spain; indeed, Spaniards consider it to be rather unattractive. The Spanish style is to take a relaxed attitude toward work and to separate it clearly from one's personal life. Spaniards often see Americans as being rather boring work machines who do not know how to balance their priorities and make time in their lives for fun (see chapter 6). Spaniards often say to Americans in Spain, "But you like it better here, don't you? Life is pleasanter here, isn't it?"

Some Spaniards feel that the long Spanish working day leads to a more relaxed attitude toward work (typical office hours are 9:00 A.M. to 1:30 or 2:00 P.M. and 4:00 P.M. to 7:00 P.M.). Whatever the reason, Spaniards certainly work at a more relaxed pace than Americans do. On arriving in the morning they catch up on the personal news of their colleagues, look at the paper, have a cup of coffee and then think about work. Sometime before lunch they start to wind down. After lunch it takes a while to start up again, and about an hour before quitting time they start to wind down again.

In the summer most offices in Spain change to *horario de verano*, or summer schedule, which usually means a six-hour workday during July and August, though some organizations start summer hours in June and do not end them until early September. The reason for this change in schedule becomes clear after you have lived in Spain awhile. First, everything slows down because of the number of people who are on vacation. The impact on business of summer vacations is greater in Spain than in the U.S. because all employees are entitled to a month's paid vacation and all vacations tend to be taken in either July or August. Second, the summer is very hot. Even air-conditioned offices cannot alleviate the searing heat of a Spanish afternoon in July or August, when the only reasonable thing for civilized human beings to do is to sleep in a room with all the shades pulled down. Because of this, Spaniards work without a break from about 9:00 A.M. to about 3:00 P.M. and then stop for the rest of the day. They cannot believe that in the U.S., despite summer temperatures in excess of one hundred degrees Fahrenheit in some places, Americans make no concessions to the heat—except to work in air-conditioned offices.

What is interesting about the summer schedule, which much more closely resembles the American working day, is that Spaniards typically work more steadily and in a more concentrated fashion during these six hours than during the two sessions of their normal working day the rest of the year. Many Spaniards prefer their summer schedule, not just because the total number of hours is shorter but also because it means they can get work over with and still have some of the day left. This seems to confirm the theory that the length of the Spanish working day contributes in part to the Spanish attitude toward work. However, one cannot help feeling that Spanish work hours may one day change, especially now that Spain has joined the European Community.

Another aspect of the work ethic that Americans and Spaniards have identified as different is the contrast between what David Riesman, a social psychologist, calls "inner direction" and "other direction." Despite the fact that many years ago Riesman argued that Americans had changed from being inner-directed to other-directed, Americans are often perceived by others, including Spaniards, as self-starters who make their own plans and maintain control over what they do, while Spaniards tend to wait to be directed. If in an office the American is the manager, it is his or her job to initiate and direct; Spaniards will wait for direction because they are subordinates. They may feel that they cannot initiate because it is not their prerogative, and they may also avoid being too self-starting because they do not want to create more work for themselves. Anyone who has worked in the U.S. is perfectly familiar with coworkers who do not take initiative or are simply not interested in their jobs. But such people are rarely sent on overseas assignments.

Thus, Americans sent abroad are likely to be highly motivated and work oriented and will probably find it difficult to get used to the relaxed Spanish style. It is their job to manage and lead, to set an example and, especially, to live up to home-office expectations. As one American pointed out, if you have been hired as a foreign expert, then you have to be a foreign expert.

Nevertheless, some adaptation is desirable, particularly in distinguishing between the goal of getting the work done according to certain standards and the *style* of getting it done; in other words, there is usually more than one way to reach a given goal.

One of the major challenges faced by the American manager in Spain is to find ways to achieve the organization's goals by incorporating Spanish culture-based work styles rather than trying to replace them with the American work ethic.

Ambition and success
Spaniards see Americans as highly ambitious, restless people who are never content with what they have, but who will sell their homes and move across the country or switch to a completely

different profession in order to satisfy those ambitions. This is not common in Spain. Spaniards say, *Somos comodones* ("We like things easy") and will not take the risks involved in making these changes. Americans view this attitude as lackadaisical, which may be in part because success for an American is highly personal and defined by the visible rewards of one's own efforts. For Spaniards success is more a matter of status, either social status or that conferred by position. A Spaniard might be impressed by a person with the title of *catedrático* (tenured professor), while an American might be more concerned with the size of the professor's salary, the number of his or her publications, and the offices held in prestigious organizations. Similarly, a Spaniard might have a hard time understanding how an American could give up a position with the title of president or director because the salary was insufficient or the work unchallenging.

For a Spaniard, success lies in the title as much as in the salary, and much more than in the work. This may be another reason why Spaniards have traditionally been loath to change jobs. The attractions of a better salary or more interesting work are outweighed by the disadvantages of having to start again and lose the status one has already achieved. Spaniards would generally rather stay in one job and wait for the promotion that will eventually arrive because of seniority. Americans are shocked when they attempt to motivate Spaniards by appealing to their ambition and find that, at least in the American sense, it is missing.

Discipline
The difference in attitudes toward self-discipline is illustrated by the experience of an American who coached a volleyball team in Murcia. She commented that Spanish players would fool around at the beginning of practice rather than getting down to drilling right away. She was also shocked that her players let emotions interfere with their game, deliberately playing badly if they were angry with the coach or the referee, for example. Finally, she complained about players showing up late not only for practice but also for matches and tournaments.

For Americans, these behaviors (lack of dedication, insufficient emotional control and failure to be punctual) demonstrate a lack of self-discipline. Americans assume that people will discipline themselves in order to achieve an objective, but Spaniards do not function that way. Whatever their objectives, they do not lose sight of or subordinate their personal feelings and inclinations. They practice until they are tired; if they are angry or upset, they show it; and punctuality, while desirable, is not an absolute value as in the U.S.

Spaniards approach work with these same attitudes. Many employees arrive late to work or slip out to do personal errands during working hours (although American managers in Spain comment that in general absenteeism is very low). In reaction to this, some offices (American and Spanish) are extremely strict. Private conversations and phone calls are absolutely forbidden, and any absence from one's desk, even to go to the bathroom, has to be justified.

American managers must tread carefully here. On the one hand, they want to see the kind of self-discipline at work that they have been used to in the U.S. On the other hand, repressive measures are undesirable anywhere, and in Spain remind people of the Franco era. Americans do best by setting an example of the type of self-discipline they expect. Then they might determine what bothers them the most and take a stand on that issue, whether it be punctuality, personal phone calls or the filling out of soccer pool forms on company time. If the one or two major irritations are removed, then the American will more easily be able to accept other, smaller annoyances.

Americans are usually astounded at the level of job security in Spain and the difficulty of firing a worker. Trade unions are active and powerful (as they are elsewhere in Europe) and have large memberships. Knowing this, Americans, upset by what they see as a lack of self-discipline and work ethic, assume there is no structure of either internal or external discipline in Spain, but such is not the case. All employees are governed by the *Estatuto del trabajador* (Workers' Code), which sets out the requirements for proper job performance, including punctuality, industriousness, working relationships, loyalty to the employer, etc. Breach of this code can lead to disciplinary action in the form of written admonitions, warnings, suspension from work, docked pay, and even dismissal. Many organizations have a *comité de empresa*, or employees' council, whose function is to inform, counsel and defend the employees but also to warn them in the case of breach of the workers' code. In sports there are also codes of behavior, and individuals or teams can be sanctioned for breaches. Every profession has its *colegio oficial* which issues licenses to individuals to practice that profession, and which receives, investigates and acts upon complaints or reports of unprofessional behavior.

Teamwork
While Spaniards and Americans do not approach teamwork in exactly the same way, the differences between them are perhaps mostly a matter of opinion, especially in contrast to other cultures, such as Japan, where there is a strong orientation toward team spirit and a collective mentality.

Some would say that Spaniards work poorly in teams. It has been remarked that Santiago Ramón y Cajal, the Spanish scientist who won the Nobel Prize for his work in endocrinology, achieved this award for work done mainly alone, without the need for a research team or a complicated support system. The implication here is that the Nobel Prize could not be reached by Spaniards in a team, only by one Spaniard alone. In an article in *El País* entitled "Why Spaniards Innovate So Little," Eduardo Punset, an economist and economic and political writer, identified teamwork as one of the prerequisites for innovation among people of like minds and like interests—something he felt to be lacking, if not in Spaniards, at least in the Spanish educational system.[4] The American volleyball coach previously mentioned found teamwork, as she expected it from her American perspective, clearly lacking in her Spanish teams.

On the other hand, Spaniards do work in teams under some circumstances. It is common, for instance, in Spanish schools and universities for students to present projects, papers and theses that are the work of a group rather than an individual. At conferences where both Spaniards and foreigners are giving presentations, it is interesting to see how many of the Spanish presentations are the work of a team, while the other presentations are usually the work of individuals.

Perhaps the major difference between Spain and the U.S. in this respect is that teamwork is actively fostered by American supervisors and managers. In the U.S. the tradition of clubs and associations as well as the national love of sports and the emphasis on sports in school, imbue Americans with a belief in the value of teamwork. This value often coexists, however, with a strong individualistic, competitive drive.

The analogy of the "winning team" is used by American managers to define optimum work relationships. Tom Peters, in his popular book on management style, *In Search of Excellence*, suggests that one of the most prominent elements contributing to the success of the best companies is that the employees think of themselves as a team and cooperate actively with one another to achieve team goals, whether related to manufacturing, customer service, sales or another function of the company.[5] Techniques used in training and development, such as Outward Bound programs in which participants learn to trust and depend on the other members of the group, are also based on "winning team" assumptions.

Though Spanish work colleagues think of themselves as members of a family, teamwork does not automatically result. A family consists of people of different ages, degrees of education, political ideas and personalities, held together by emotional and blood ties. A team, on the other hand, usually consists of selected people with similar or complementary education, skills, background and goals. The Spanish relationship of *familia* at work, like that of the family at home, is to a great extent an emotional one with ties that stem from shared experiences, long acquaintance and personal attachment.

American managers, teachers or coaches who come to work in Spain will probably find that team building is needed. Spaniards, for their part, should probably expect American managers to be concerned with teamwork, since this is one of the well-known canons of modern American management style.

However, once again, Americans should not attempt simply to transplant ideas wholesale. Of the Spaniards interviewed for this book who had read *In Search of Excellence*, all felt that while it was interesting, its ideas could not be transferred indiscriminately to Spain.

Competitiveness

The American belief in individualism goes hand in hand with a strong competitive spirit. The achievement of an individual is valued above the harmony of the group, and individualism and competitiveness are both seen as positive. In Spain, however, both individualism and competitiveness are seen as actually or potentially negative. Competitiveness, in particular, is associated with envidia, "the Spanish vice."

American bosses should be wary of fostering what they see as "healthy competition," as one American executive found out when he attempted to hire someone for the newly created position of controller in the Spanish branch of a growing multinational company. Wanting to fill the job from inside, the American identified three people as likely candidates. He then decided to observe each of them for six months, evaluate their performance over that period, and only then make the appointment. He next called in each of the three, told them of the availability of the job and informed them of his plans. So far, so good. But he then also told each of them who the other two candidates were and that they were in open competition. That was his mistake.

Earlier, his secretary had tried in vain to persuade him not to declare the competition open. "No, no," said the American, "That's the way I would do it in the States and that's the way I'm going to do it here. They'll work harder and show their best." Unfortunately, the results were not what he expected. One of the candidates, the best of the three, resigned on the spot, saying that he refused to be a part of what was going to happen. The other two candidates tore each other to shreds, using every possible stratagem to strengthen their own positions and weaken the competitor's. At the end of six months, one of them was appointed controller and the other promptly resigned. Thus the company lost two out of three good people and suffered the consequences of open warfare carried out over the fateful period. It is to the credit of the CEO that he privately admitted his error, but the damage had already been done.

The moral of this story is that competition is not the same for a Spaniard as for an American. For Americans it is generally assumed to be positive, healthy and a normal part of working life. For Spaniards, it is often negative and destructive and an invitation to *envidia*. Americans should be wary of using individual competition to motivate people, both inside the organization and out.

Growth

Spanish businesses have traditionally not felt compelled to compete, grow and excel to the same extent as American companies. U.S. business publications devote a lot of attention to takeovers, mergers, ambitious expansion plans and other manifestations of a drive to be the best. Growth is, of course, desirable to a Spanish business, and there are upwardly mobile heroes such as the young businessman who by his early twenties had already built up a highly successful chain of clothing stores. However, a person who is carrying on a centuries-old family concern, whether hotel, restaurant, vineyard or factory, is also admired in Spain. Spaniards are just as impressed by a business that has been in operation for one or two hundred years and hasn't changed appreciably as by one that was started only a few years back and has performed spectacularly.

However, the lack of drive to compete, grow and excel poses a problem for the future of Spanish business. In the post-1992 unified European market, economic commentators have pointed to the relative unpreparedness of much of Spanish business to deal with competition from the rest of Europe as protectionist trade barriers come down. National and local governments and, to a lesser extent, chambers of commerce and trade organizations have taken it upon themselves to set goals for Spanish business. The Socialist government that was elected overwhelmingly in 1982 and reelected in 1986 and 1989 took advantage of its broad support base and highly skilled and well-connected technocrats to push the country firmly in the direction of change.

Work Environment

Hierarchy

Americans interviewed for this book generally said that they found Spaniards more conscious of hierarchy than Americans. Spaniards said that most Americans seemed less status-conscious than Spaniards. It may be that these Spaniards were simply reacting to the friendly, up-front image projected by many Americans and that this friendliness obscures the fact that Americans are in fact quite status-conscious, though in ways different from the Spanish.

In any event it appears that the source of status differs between the two countries. While for Americans it is based on achievement and material possessions, for Spaniards it is related much more to position, title and public image. Pride and honor have been recurrent themes in Spanish literature. Foreigners, from respected historians to popular novelists and commentators such as James Michener, have often taken note of the importance of pride in the Spanish psyche. Some historians trace it back to the reconquest and the preoccupation with being *hidalgo*, that is, "somebody" (literally, the son of somebody). It is probably questionable whether a modern Spanish man working in a multinational corporation is preoccupied with being an hidalgo, but he undoubtedly has a clear idea of who he is and what is due him according to his status.

Putting oneself in the Spaniard's place may help Americans to be more tactful than one high-level American manager whose corporation had offices in both Barcelona and Madrid. This manager visited the Barcelona office and then, to save time, had Barcelona set up interviews with various influential businesspeople and public figures in Madrid. He thus bypassed completely the head of the Madrid office (the most senior person in the corporate hierarchy) who, on hearing of the scheduled interviews from the people who had been contacted, summarily canceled them. The visitor's behavior was very American in placing speed and convenience over considerations of hierarchy; the Madrid boss's reaction was very Spanish in placing personal honor and considerations of hierarchy over efficiency.

Authority and respect

What is particularly striking about the preceding anecdote is that it contrasts sharply with what is normally an ingrained respect for authority in Spain. Politeness is often defined in terms of respect; to be rude in Castilian is *faltar al respeto* (literally, to be lacking in respect). Spaniards are brought up to respect people who are older or in authority. In turn, they expect respect from those who they feel owe it to them. This system of respect is by no means as strong as in Japan or some Arab cultures, but it is certainly stronger than in the U.S., where one of the basic tenets of the culture is social equality and where being overly respectful still carries a connotation of inequality. Americans are usually very conscious of their rights as individuals; they are quick to speak up in meetings and make their opinions heard, or readily approach people in authority to talk about things that are bothering them. Americans discuss problems with their supervisors or express discontent with levels of pay, working conditions or anything else that is not to their liking. Spaniards are not so quick to do this, perhaps because of respect or because of cynicism about the results that are likely to be achieved.

Americans in a work situation with Spaniards notice that they are less likely to speak up in meetings, write petitions or letters, or solicit interviews in which to talk over problems. Seeing this,

Americans may assume—wrongly—that Spaniards have no opinions, or are unconcerned about public or personal problems, or perhaps are still living with the effects of forty years of dictatorship (or even that the forty years of dictatorship were made possible by just such passivity). What is true is that Spaniards are concerned with being subtle and with choosing the right time to speak in order to ensure that they do not make themselves or their colleagues look foolish. Spaniards are in general afraid of looking foolish (*hacer el ridículo*) and will go to a lot of trouble to avoid it. They may prefer to state their opinions in private to the person concerned rather than in an open meeting, or wait and see what time will bring if they remain silent, or perhaps enlist the support of the comité de empresa, a neutral body whose function it is to express their opinions for them.

Business education

One clear difference between Americans and Spaniards in business is that Spaniards do not have access to the kind of practical information that American business executives receive as a matter of course. Excellent management training programs, both full- and part-time, are offered at Spanish universities and private schools. However, most of the people engaged in small or medium-sized businesses either learned on the job without formal training or, if they have college degrees, majored in such subjects as economics, philosophy, law or political science. There is no equivalent of the Small Business Administration or university extension services to make available practical information on business management. Corporate training is in its infancy. All of this means that people in small and medium-sized businesses have practical experience and expertise but are lacking in basic business education. Also, even though there are trade organizations, chambers of commerce, trade shows and specialized business and technical publications, Spanish managers are often cut off, not only from information, but also from the motivation to grow which that information brings.

Work Styles

Goals

In multinational corporations or those most influenced by modern American business practices, corporate goal setting is an important part of management. However, in Spanish organizations it often seems that clear goals are not set; instead, it is assumed that the goals for the next year or the next few years will be the same as in the past. A number of factors are probably responsible for this. First, a large number of companies and organizations in Spain are not only small but are also run by families. Staff may consist entirely of family members or employees who have been around so long they have come to be regarded as such. In small businesses of this kind anywhere in the world, goal setting (which implies change) may be the dream of the restless younger members of the family but is resisted by the conservative older members who can't see why things should be done differently. Even in a spanking new video club, croissant shop or restaurant recently opened by young people, there may be no clear or formally established goals other than to keep going month to month and year to year.

Rewards and promotions

Personal goal setting by employees may be found in multinationals, but one would have to look a long time before finding it in most Spanish organizations, large or small. There seem to be two main reasons for this. First, in a hierarchical society with status based on position, subordinates are not often encouraged to think for themselves or to set their own goals, which can be seen as a way of defining and influencing both their roles in the organization and the organization itself. Spanish superiors are often simply too autocratic to allow this type of autonomous thinking in their subordinates. Secondly, in the U.S. the practice of personal goal setting is usually tied in with some kind of reward system based on an appraisal of the employee's performance in relation to corporate—and sometimes personal—goals.

Rewards in the form of money or promotion for work well done are taken for granted. This assumes, first, that the pay policies of the organization provide for financial rewards and, second, that the personnel structure provides for promotions. It also implies that organizations need to offer such rewards to valuable employees in order to ensure they are not enticed away by some competing organization.

These three assumptions are probably what make the U.S. the land of milk and honey in the minds of many Spaniards. In Spain pay structures in businesses resemble those in government, where raises are often negotiated on a national basis once a year and are strictly tied to status within the organization. Promotions are also often determined by seniority or loyalty as much as (or more than) high performance. Further, with the job situation being so tight, employers know that the danger of losing good employees is slim, and the need to provide inducements for them to stay is correspondingly less pressing. Recognizing these conditions may help Americans understand why Spaniards sometimes appear unambitious and not identified with their work.

Decision making and problem solving
The greater consciousness of status and hierarchy in Spain reflects and reinforces a more autocratic management style than Americans are used to. This difference also shows up in problem-solving and decision-making styles. In a Spanish organization the line of authority is likely to be top-down, with the highest person in the hierarchy making the decisions essentially alone. One result is that Spanish managers frequently make a decision and then have to rescind or modify it because of protests or pressures from people affected. Workers may strike or threaten to strike and customers or constituents may raise a hue and cry.

American decision making is top-down too (in contrast, for example, to the Japanese, whose bottom-up, consensus style of decision making is now famous), but they are much more inclined to consult, gather other opinions and test the waters than Spanish executives.

But Americans, for all their friendly ways and easy consultations, surprise Spaniards with their ability to make drastic decisions with severe effects. They will, for example, close an unprofitable branch office, which puts people out of work, under circumstances where Spaniards might hesitate. Spaniards are likely to be influenced by tradition, human factors or simple unwillingness to make an unpopular decision.

Planning, details and systems

When President Ronald Reagan visited Madrid in May 1985, he was preceded by the usual advance team whose job it was to make sure everything had been properly planned and would run smoothly. An article in *El País* covering preparations for the president's visit commented on *el prolijo detallismo de los americanos* (the Americans' unlimited passion for details), which was driving Spanish counterparts to distraction.

Not long afterward the prime minister of Spain, Felipe González, made an official visit to China, accompanied by numerous government officials and prominent businesspeople. The purpose of the visit was both political and economic, and it was one of the most significant foreign trips of González's first administration. To the consternation of Spaniards (Chinese reactions were not reported), the government mission arrived in Beijing some six hours late, causing all the welcoming ceremonies and the official banquet to be postponed and the schedule for the entire visit to be altered. The reason: the prime minister's plane had to make an unexpected detour. Someone had failed to obtain permission for the plane to cross the airspace of a Middle Eastern country. A little detallismo would not have been amiss here.

Spaniards think that Americans worry too much about details, are obsessively pessimistic (saying "What if...?" too much) and want to have everything nailed down. They also fuss if anything is late, misplaced or confused. Americans think that Spaniards leave far too much to chance, work out only the general outlines of a plan and none of the details, don't consider the possibility that something might go wrong, and are often late, misplaced or confused.

The American concern with detail is closely allied to the American predilection for systems, with everything clearly labeled and under control. They like information and a lot of it and do not like being in doubt or being taken by surprise. One Spaniard being interviewed for this book smiled at the very idea of its being written. "You are writing a handbook," he said, "something dear to the hearts of Americans, full of detailed information that will make things clear and lessen ambiguity and confusion."

While they often admire the results, Spaniards find American *detallismo* unnerving, and if they are expected to display the same attention to detail because of an American boss or rules from American headquarters, it takes considerable adaptation on their part. Americans who have adapted to Spanish ways have come to accept that details may not be attended to, that information may not always be exact, and that they have to loosen up a little and not fuss so much.

Spaniards rely on chance or luck much more than Americans do. While lotteries are increasing in popularity in the U.S., they can't match Spain, where they are a national addiction. There are half a dozen different lotteries in which people participate on a regular basis. Lottery ticket sellers wander through bars and restaurants carrying sheaves of tickets, and it seems that on every street corner there is a lottery ticket booth. The Spanish also depend on *suerte* (luck) more than Americans do, whether referring to exam results (Americans would think they should have studied harder), finding a hotel room (Americans would think they should have called ahead) or talking their way around a regulation (Americans would think they should take no for an answer).

Trusting to luck is not compatible with thinking that something might go wrong. Americans generally have a contingency plan worked out in case something goes awry, so that when it does, there is an alternative course of action already determined which enables the problem to be solved quickly and painlessly. In Spain there is usually no contingency plan, which means that dealing with problems creates a lot more confusion and emotion. People get tense and start raising their voices. Even a relatively minor hitch, which is usually solvable without too much difficulty, is accompanied in Spain by a chorus of angry words, raised voices, mutterings and threats which, in the U.S., would generally denote a much more serious breakdown in the system. On one occasion at New York's Kennedy Airport, two Spanish executives were waiting at the Iberia desk to have their connecting flights rescheduled because of the delayed arrival of their flight from Spain. The desk was swamped with passengers, some of them irate, and all needing to be rescheduled, which was handled by the American staff with quiet efficiency. When his turn came, one of the Spanish executives murmured to the other, *Son apagados, pero van haciendo* ("They're very low-key, but they get on with the job"). He was struck by the absence of fuss in what was potentially an emotional, if not explosive, situation.

On the other hand, Spaniards are concerned that too much planning leads to loss of spontaneity and flexibility. Americans sometimes seem to Spaniards too hung up on their own plans and systems and unable or unwilling to deviate from them in order to solve a problem. "Strict" and "inflexible" are adjectives that Spaniards often use about Americans, especially when adherence to a plan or system ignores the personal impact it has on those involved. This excessive commitment to plans and systems is somewhat of a paradox, since Americans tend to pride themselves on their flexibility and are quite willing to change plans if it helps to solve problems. But changes for other reasons are not well received. The more vigorously the Americans pursue their plans and implement their systems, the more the Spaniards push them to be flexible, which in turn causes the Americans to stiffen up and become extremely annoyed at what they consider slapdash Spanish attitudes.

A related issue is the Spanish disregard for danger. Startling to the cautious American, it is most apparent on the road. Spaniards drive much faster and take more risks than do Americans, and the toll of their reckless abandon is reflected, in part, by the terrible statistics of traffic deaths. Americans cite bull-fighting as an example of the Spanish cult of death and danger. In the industrial workplace the American preoccupation with protective clothing, heavy shoes, goggles and head coverings is regarded by many Spaniards as obsessive and pusillanimous. Spaniards prefer to forge ahead, assuming nothing will go wrong. Regrettably, Americans find this approach so unnerving that their reaction is to reject out of hand things made and done by Spaniards; they refuse treatment by Spanish doctors and dentists and denigrate Spanish workmanship.

Negotiating

Spaniards comment on the American propensity for getting to the point (*ir al grano* in Spanish). Most Spaniards regard this as a positive attribute in conducting meetings or in writing letters and reports, in contrast with their own tendency to long-windedness. But when an American first encounters a Spaniard, especially in a business negotiation, getting to the point too rapidly can be a hindrance rather than a help. When Spaniards meet someone for the first time to plan, bargain or negotiate, they want to take the measure of their counterpart and decide whether they would like to do business with him or her. Americans want to know the same thing, but they feel they can accomplish it while discussing the business at hand. The Spaniard would rather get acquainted by discussing world politics or soccer or the beauty of the Pyrenees. Americans are impatient with this type of conversation (which they are inclined to see as beating around the bush or wasting time), but those who do not take the time to get acquainted are likely to appear boorish and abrasive.

Ironically, Americans may leave such an encounter feeling quite satisfied, since Spanish courtesy demands that they follow the lead of the American and, in addition, not show their displeasure. But the Americans in such encounters may have set a time bomb for themselves that will jeopardize future interaction. McCaffrey and Haffner suggest that this kind of behavior constitutes a "false efficiency," since it does not provide for the development of the understanding and trust needed when entering a business relationship.[6] It also results in missed opportunities because of failure to pick up on subtle signals during early encounters.

One example of this false efficiency occurred when a young, eager American executive in a multinational firm called on a potential Spanish client. This client lived in a city about a hundred miles away, and since there were no good air connections, it was arranged that the executive would be chauffeured to the meeting in the company car. On arrival, the driver went off to the men's room and to stretch his legs. When he returned fifteen minutes later, he found the American seated in the car waiting to be driven back. The driver was astounded, and so, no doubt, was the client, who must certainly have expected a wide-ranging discussion lasting one or two hours, probably followed by lunch. No acquaintanceship of any kind could be made in fifteen minutes, and certainly no business matters of any substance could be broached. All the executive seemed to accomplish was to reinforce the image of the time-obsessed American that the Spaniard already had. The driver, of course, regaled the entire company with the story.

The conflict between conciseness and long-windedness does not end once the American and Spanish parties begin discussing the business at hand. Americans usually try to present their information and proposals in a brief, sequential and neatly packaged form. Spaniards, in contrast, are usually not brief. They discuss things at length, often repeating themselves two or three times. Apparently unrelated information or references are brought in, providing the discussion with more ramifications than Americans are usually ready for.

If disagreement arises during the negotiations, Spaniards are likely to raise their voices. In Spanish conversation, turn taking is less strictly observed than in the U.S. Spaniards interrupt speakers without intending offense, and speakers raise their voices in the face of attempted interruption or disagreement. Therefore, Spanish negotiations, like Spanish conversation, can easily become loud. Americans, who value a controlled and dispassionate demeanor in professional situations, are distressed by loud voices, which they interpret as anger, and by interruptions, which they interpret as rudeness.

Disagreement may seem to be anger, both because of the volume and also because Spaniards do not lightly concede points in a discussion or argument. Americans, believing that discussions are sequential, tend to believe that if one is won over to the opposing view, it will be through logic, point by point. However, Spaniards, when faced with opposition, are likely to restate their own point more forcefully, appearing to be categorically rejecting any alternative. Americans should avoid the urge to give up when such obstacles arise. While they may see the negotiation as a road with a series of milestones, the Spaniards see it more as a clearing in the forest. Agreement is often not reached point by point, but rather in general terms once all the factors have been discussed from every angle.

Finally, when agreement is reached, Spaniards often leave details undecided. Americans should remember the example of Spanish legislation. First comes the *ley* (law) and then the *reglamento* (regulation), which sets out all the details. The two are not forthcoming simultaneously. Similarly, the outcome of negotiation with Spaniards may be general principles rather than details. Americans who wish to save future headaches and/or indulge their passion for detallismo may find several follow-up meetings to be necessary.

6

Play

The Paradox

Both Spaniards and Americans, in Spain and in the U.S., comment that while Spaniards work longer days, they seem to have more fun. Spaniards who have moved to the U.S. usually bewail the fact that their lives seem to consist of going from work to home and from home to work. They hark back to the good old days in Spain, while Americans who move back to the U.S. after living in Spain also complain of the monotony of American life and wax nostalgic for the Spanish lifestyle.

Mythmaking is at work here. Most Spaniards certainly do not go out and whoop it up every night. They are more likely to go straight home from work, have dinner with the family and watch TV until bedtime. An American in Spain on vacation may be misled by the summer atmosphere, where even those people who are working are on reduced hours and are therefore free to stroll or barhop in the evenings. Meanwhile, Spaniards who criticize the "home-to-work-to-home" monotony of American workers often fail to realize how many activities in the U.S. take place after dinner. "After dinner" to a Spaniard means about 11:00 P.M.; Spaniards who have something to do in the evening generally postpone dinner until it is over.

Spaniards (and Americans in Spain) seem to have more fun, which many attribute to greater spontaneity in the Spanish personality. The American passion for detail tends to carry over into social life, so that they plan their play as thoroughly as they plan their work. Spaniards in the U.S. often comment that in order to get together socially with Americans you have to organize it weeks ahead "and write everything down in a little appointment book." Americans new to Spain take a vague "Let's do something on Tuesday night" for a firm commitment and may be annoyed or hurt if nothing materializes when Tuesday night arrives. However, Americans are charmed by the Spanish talent for arranging an outing on the spur of the moment or creating a fiesta out of nothing. Times have changed little since Margaret Fountaine, a Victorian traveler and butterfly collector, visited Spain in the early years of this century.

> The train was more than an hour late, and while we were waiting one man played a guitar, while I, at the urgent request of the assembled company, danced with the *jefe de estación* [stationmaster] in spite of limited space and mountain shoes.[7]

It is also easier to be spontaneous with Spaniards because they are not hung up about going to bed early in order to get up for work the next day. All foreigners (not just Americans) are bemused by the small amount of sleep Spaniards find sufficient. An article once appeared in a Spanish women's magazine discussing stress and simple remedies for dealing with it. On the subject of sleep the advice was *Trata de dormir seis horas* (Make a point of getting six hours' sleep). This implied that even in modern, siesta-less times, six hours' sleep per night, which most Americans would consider to be one or two hours short of the minimum, was regarded by Spaniards as being more than normal and something to strive for. Certainly a Spaniard would never cut short an enjoyable evening in order to go to bed. *Un día es un día* (Live for today), Spaniards say, and it is this attitude that makes Spain fun.

Holidays and Vacations

Spaniards, like many other foreigners, think of the U.S. as the land of plenty and of opportunity. However, when Spaniards find out about American vacations, they are stunned. The American two-week annual vacation contrasts poorly indeed with the month (not four weeks) that Spaniards, along with other Europeans, expect as their normal due. "Two weeks!" say Spaniards in horror. "How can anyone manage on only two weeks' vacation a year?"

In addition to the annual paid vacation (and to the reduced summer work schedule), Spaniards also enjoy a good number of holidays throughout the year. Religious dates such as Christmas, Good Friday and Assumption of the Virgin are celebrated throughout Spain. The Easter holiday, famous for the processions in Seville and elsewhere, stretches from Thursday to Sunday or Monday. Cities and regions have their patron saints with corresponding holidays, which vary from one place to another. There are also secular holidays such as Columbus Day and Constitution Day.

What is interesting, and for Americans very different, is the way in which Spaniards use their time off. One American man married to a Spanish woman described Spanish leisure in a moment of frustration as "the concept of life as ritual." In the U.S., the most ritualized holiday is probably Thanksgiving. Football, turkey, pumpkin pie and family reunions are the norms of Thanksgiving. No other nonreligious holiday is quite so clearly defined, since at other times one may celebrate or not, get together with the family or not, and eat whatever seems tasty or appropriate. To Americans, it often seems that Spaniards have a Thanksgiving-type ritual for all their holidays. On holidays, as on Sundays, Spaniards get up late, put on their best clothes in late morning and go out for a walk with the family, which ends with prelunch drinks and snacks at a café. Then comes a big lunch at a restaurant or at the home of a family member, and then everyone watches the movie special on TV or goes out to see a movie or attend some event. Naturally, not every Spaniard spends holidays in this way, but it is overwhelmingly the norm. Many Americans live so far from their families that they cannot possibly spend every Sunday or holiday together. Nor is distance the only factor. Many Americans would regard such close family contact, and particularly spending so much precious free time with family, as an intrusion on their own individuality and their right to spend their holiday as they please. Perhaps it is because Americans have less free time that they often take the attitude that it must be used productively. For Spaniards, free time is not regarded as such a precious commodity, and, in particular, time spent with family is not time to be accounted for.

Social Life

What Spaniards actually do for entertainment in their free time and in socializing with friends is similar to what Americans do: going out for *tapas* (varied snacks to accompany drinks), for dinner, for after-dinner drinks and maybe dancing. Americans usually have no problem in relating to this, and many an American love affair with Spain (or with a Spaniard) has begun with a social evening.

One feature of Spanish social life which impresses and sometimes embarrasses Americans is the openhanded generosity of Spaniards. Fernando Diaz-Plaja in *The Spaniard and the Seven Deadly Sins* dedicates one short chapter to the sin of avarice, just long enough to say that Spaniards do not suffer from it.[8] This is absolutely true, and nothing shocks a Spaniard more than to see Americans nickeling and diming about who owes what when they are out together. Spaniards are likely to argue about who gets to pick up the whole tab. *Te invito* ("You're my guest"), says the Spaniard, snatching up the bill and refusing to allow others to contribute unless it is a very large party. Only Catalans, who have a reputation in Spain for closefistedness, are likely to agree to dividing the bill. Americans sometimes think that Spaniards are trying to show off by making a display of big spending. This is not the case; hospitality in this sense is both generous and reciprocal. I pay for you this time and you pay for me next time.

Generosity extends not only to formal dinners but to something as minor as a cup of coffee or a soft drink. In one of the most common traveler's tales about Spain, the travelers start talking to Spaniards in a bar or restaurant and find when they come to pay that the bill has already been taken care of. This is a basic courtesy in Spain and must be accepted graciously, like invitations to have something to drink. *¿Quiere tomar algo?* ("Would you like to have something?") is an automatic question when the conversation is taking place in a café or bar. Business offices have a place to make coffee or will send out for it so that they can offer something to clients when the occasion seems to demand it. Americans may respond according to whether they really want a cup of coffee or a cool drink, but for a Spaniard it is next to impossible to say no when someone says, "¿Quiere tomar algo?"

One striking difference between American and Spanish custom is that much if not most of Spanish social life takes place outside the home. Groups of friends who have made arrangements to spend some time together usually meet at a public place such as a café (and every city has a café that is the favorite meeting place). Then the group goes on to a restaurant, a show, a nightclub or wherever they have decided. Once again, when a group of Spaniards arranges to meet at a fixed place and time, anything up to an hour may elapse between the arrival of the first person and the arrival of the last. If Americans are involved in one of these groups, they are typically the first to arrive, so they end up waiting the longest until everyone has arrived. Then comes the final straw: one of the Spaniards says *¿Qué hacemos?* ("What shall we do?"). Much discussion ensues, probably with the Americans glancing at their watches and thinking crossly about the amount of time being wasted. Americans who have adapted to Spain learn to arrive sometime after the fixed hour and to realize that the question "¿Qué hacemos?" is largely rhetorical and is asked even though plans for the evening are already fairly firm, in order to make it clear that any member of the group can still make changes or suggestions.

While Americans might meet at someone's home and go on from there, or maybe go home for coffee or drinks after a social event, Spaniards normally do not expect to go to someone's home for a social gathering. Usually only family members and close friends come to one's home; and parties such as Americans often give are practically unknown. There are several explanations for this: one is that there is a clear division (often attributed to the Moorish influence) in Spain between the privacy of home and the outside world.*

Another reason, which is probably more practical, is that since many Spanish households consist of an extended family, there is not much extra room for inviting people in, and other members of the family may be disturbed by the presence of guests. Finally, Spaniards are house-proud. Only family and intimate friends are allowed to see the debris of normal living. Naturally, this is also true of Americans, who prefer that outsiders not see the house looking like a disaster area, but Spaniards feel more strongly the need to keep up appearances. Americans should respect this and realize that, at least initially, they are unlikely to see the inside of many Spanish homes.

Peace and quiet versus ambiente

The bustle of European cities is one of the things that impresses visiting Americans. Spanish cities and towns are no exception. One of the reasons for the activity is the much greater amount of foot traffic in a Spanish city than in an American one. As noted before, Spanish cities are densely built up; almost everyone lives in apartment buildings that have stores and offices on the ground

---

*Spaniards change their clothes completely when they get home (instead of just kicking off their shoes, like many Americans). One reason for this is that there is a greater preoccupation with being well turned out when one leaves the house. Clothes worn outside are too good for slopping around the house in.

floor. Even small towns and villages are constructed this way, with houses and building facades against the sidewalk and any yard space concealed behind the building. To the visiting Spaniard, an American suburb or small town seems deserted—*No hay nadie en la calle* ("There's nobody about"), they say. They often feel lonely and are bored at first in American communities, because there is not enough *ambiente*. The literal meaning of this is "atmosphere," but it usually means people and activity.

When Spaniards have nothing to do, they generally go out to do it; when Americans have nothing to do it seems that they stay home and turn on the TV. The couch potato is an American vegetable; Spaniards with time on their hands change their clothes and go out. Staying home to watch TV is generally a family activity, for example, after the big Sunday lunch.

Other people are an important source of entertainment for Spaniards, who engage in people watching to an extent that Americans find embarrassing. In Spain, it is not rude at all. Every Spanish apartment, even the poorest, has a balcony from which one can look out. People who sit at sidewalk cafés watch the people walking by, who in turn watch them. When the city is quiet on a Sunday, one has only to go to the nearest seaside or country resort to find all the missing activity, transferred along with the people.

Hobbies and sports

American sports lovers will find kindred spirits in Spain. On Monday mornings most men on the subway or bus are reading one of the specialized sporting newspapers or the sports section of the daily paper. Weekend afternoons and some weeknights are punctuated by the roars of armchair spectators as their teams score. When there is a really big game, goals are heralded by rockets that are kept in readiness and set off from rooftops or balconies.

Similar also to the U.S. is the level of sports activity among teenagers. It is only recently that sports have been readily available to all schoolchildren and particularly to girls. A generation ago sports for girls was virtually unknown. Times have changed and so have attitudes, but Spaniards are still less fitness oriented than Americans, though aerobics, racquetball and fitness centers have all hit Spain with the same impact as in the U.S.

Hobbies are an area of difference between Spaniards and Americans. For one thing, "hobby" cannot be translated into Castilian except by the word *pasatiempo*, which, like its English counterpart, "pastime," implies not so much a creative and ongoing activity as a pleasant way of spending some odd moments. Spanish people with hobbies usually use the English word to refer to them. There are, as in the U.S., collectors of stamps, coins, antiques and butterflies; nature lovers who pick mushrooms or wild asparagus; hikers and mountain climbers; people who keep pigeons and those who fly gliders. But there are probably fewer craft-type hobbies. A gap has developed between the older generation of women who knitted, crocheted and sewed (often from necessity) and the younger generation who rarely engage in these pursuits. In the U.S., this gap is often filled by crafts such as stenciling, quilt making, weaving, spinning and so on, but in Spain this is not so. The same applies to home activities such as food preserving or carpentry. In Spain, people feel that it is a waste of time to make something that can easily be bought. Many writers attribute Spanish disrespect for manual skills to the Moorish past. Whether this is a true assessment or not, the fact is that an American who weaves or stencils or does home improvements will be regarded by Spaniards as rather eccentric, perhaps to be admired but not to be emulated.

Clubs and associations

Local papers in the U.S. are full of announcements of meetings of clubs and associations, ranging in focus from historical societies to support groups for people who are ill or distressed. Furthermore, these clubs are often highly organized, with minutes of each meeting, officers and committees for each activity, and sometimes even an in-house parliamentarian to keep track of the motions, debates and votes. All this seems to tie in with the American notion of leisure time as something that must be productive.

Spaniards are much less likely to get involved in clubs and associations. There are sporting, social and professional associations, but not nearly so many as in the United States. Americans sometimes see this as another sign of a lack of community spirit among Spaniards.

It must be remembered that the right to associate was one of the rights that was curtailed, or at least supervised, during the strictest era of the Franco dictatorship. Even with the *apertura* (liberalization) of the early seventies, associations continued to be suspect as possible breeding grounds for dissent; many associations were in fact connected with some kind of ideology. Youth clubs might be closely allied with the church, or hiking clubs with some political movement. The Barcelona soccer association (*Club de Futbol Barcelona* or *Barça*) is famous for having been *més que un club* (more than a club)—a vehicle for Catalan nationalism. At a time when people still were not allowed to speak Catalan and regional autonomy was still a dream, Catalan songs were sung at Barça games, and Barça victories were a source of pride to more than soccer fans. Because of the experience of the last two generations, most Spaniards are not in the habit of belonging to clubs or associations, and, if they thought about it, would probably reject the idea because of not wanting to get involved in something bigger or more complicated than the name and professed aims of the group might suggest.

Conclusion: Encounters

As a conclusion, this section presents a series of encounters between Spaniards and Americans that can cause misunderstanding, embarrassment or conflict.

Business Dealings

Peter works for the Acme Company at its Minneapolis office. Acme manufactures some of its products in Spain for the European market. Peter is on a trip to Spain, visiting the Spanish operation and looking into the possibility of expanding the manufacturing and distribution activities. The Spanish manager has made contact with several top executives in industry and banking and has arranged meetings with them. How much preliminary general conversation should Peter expect at each meeting?

  A. ten minutes.

  B. twenty minutes.

  C. thirty minutes.

—————————————

A *would be a short time unless the Spaniard knows that Americans like to get to the point.*

B *is the average time spent.*

C *is also reasonable.*

Peter's counterpart in his first meeting turns out to have spent his high school junior year in the Twin Cities, so preliminary chat lasts over half an hour. When the topic of the meeting is finally broached, Peter, with an inward sigh of relief, produces the relevant documents. Though a great deal more discussion ensues, Peter is dismayed that many specifics are not addressed. Finally realizing that only twenty minutes of the appointed time remain, Peter starts pressing for firm answers to some of his specific questions. His counterpart answers vaguely and glances at Peter's Spanish manager, who hastily brings the meeting to a close. Can this meeting be considered a success?

Yes, for the first meeting. Rapport has been established and the general outlines of the topic have been discussed. There will be time for details later. Nonetheless, if Peter is responsible for those details, in later meetings he will have to insist (politely) on answers, since Spaniards are frequently far more comfortable than Americans with vague generalities.

110

Te Invito

Jane, a sports coach, meets one of her Spanish students, MariCarmen, on the street. After a few minutes of conversation, Jane proposes they go to the café for a cup of coffee and a croissant. After chatting for almost an hour, Jane finally asks for the bill. When the waiter brings it, Jane starts doing some quick arithmetic to figure out each person's share. Suddenly, MariCarmen reaches into her purse and hands the waiter some money. She then stands up and says, *Vamos?* Jane tries to give MariCarmen enough money to cover her share, but MariCarmen brushes away the offer. They part soon afterward, with Jane feeling uncomfortable, aware that she has mishandled the event. What went wrong?

Spaniards seldom split a bill for something as small as coffee and croissants for two. Normally, one or the other would pick up the tab. MariCarmen expected Jane to pay, since she proposed the refreshments. A Spaniard in Jane's position would have said "Te invito" to forestall any misunderstanding. When Jane did not offer to pay, MariCarmen felt obliged to do so.

Ya Me lo Pagará Mañana

Michael goes to the neighborhood bakery early one Saturday morning and chooses two loaves of bread and some pastries. Reaching into his pocket, he finds that he has no change, only a single large bill. The shopkeeper is also short of change and hands him the bread and the cash register receipt, saying, "Ya me lo pagará mañana."

Michael should

A. wait to pay until his next weekly shopping trip.

B. find a way to break his large bill, get some change and pay within the hour.

C. make a point of paying within the next day or two.

D. forget about paying, since the shopkeeper obviously considers the amount trivial.

———————

A *is acceptable—just. A week is a long time to wait before paying.*

B *is not necessary. If Michael comes back to pay immediately, people will protest that he should not have bothered but at the same time they will characterize him as particularly polite and thoughtful.*

C *is the option that Spaniards would choose.*

D *is definitely wrong. The shopkeeper does not regard as trivial either the amount of money or the confianza shown in giving Michael credit. Failing to pay will make him a "marked man" in the neighborhood.*

112

Where Shall We Meet?

David plays volleyball every Saturday with a group of young men (coworkers and their friends). After a few weeks of this, someone proposes that the group get together on Sunday for lunch and a movie afterward. Where will they meet?

A. at a conveniently located café.

B. at the restaurant where they will have lunch.

C. at the home of one of the group members.

D. at David's home.

———————————

A *is the most likely option.*

B *is possible, but people usually like to get together before lunch for drinks somewhere else.*

C *is very unlikely. Most young men live at home with their families and would not be comfortable introducing a group of strangers into the privacy of the family home.*

D *is a reasonable option, but most Spaniards will not expect it.*

COMMENT: The proposal that the group meet for a purpose other than their volleyball game is a sign that the relationship is progressing. If David does propose that the group meet at his home, most Spaniards will be flattered at this sign of confianza.

The Stranger

Ben moves into his new apartment in a Spanish city. He soon locates a tobacco shop and goes in to buy stamps, carrying a stack of postcards and letters to mail to people back home. He is waited on by an attractive, well-dressed young woman. Impressed by her appearance, Ben tries out his best Spanish and all his charm, but her manner remains cool and distant. Though she has to spend some time weighing the letters and looking up the postal rates, she does not ask him where he is from or what he is doing in Spain. However, while waiting on him she greets other customers with a smile. How should Ben interpret the shop assistant's behavior?

A. she doesn't like Americans.

B. she is offended by his imperfect Spanish.

C. she is a rude and unfriendly person.

D. she doesn't know him.

A is possible, but there is no reason to assume this.

B is unlikely, since Spaniards are not touchy about foreigners speaking their language.

C is a reasonable option only if the shop assistant is judged by American expectations.

D is the most likely reason, especially as the assistant is only chilly with Ben and is friendly with other customers.

COMMENT: The shop assistant, a young and attractive single woman, would not be friendly to any stranger, particularly a male. Asking personal questions is generally avoided in Spain, and more so as she is not trying to strike up an acquaintanceship. She feels much more obligated to her regular customers, who are already being made to wait because she has to take so much time with Ben. He is likely to receive more amiable treatment once he, too, becomes a regular customer.

114

Sobre las Ocho

Judy, an American in Spain, has arranged to meet some Spanish acquaintances at a café. The plan for the evening is to have a bite to eat and then go to the movie at 10:30 P.M. The group has agreed to meet at the café *sobre las ocho* ("at around 8:00"). Judy should arrive

A. early, so as to hold a table for the group.

B. at 8:00 on the dot, as arranged.

C. between 8:00 and 8:30.

D. no earlier than 9:00, since Spaniards are always late.

A   is a fine solution if Judy does not mind waiting. The group will appreciate her holding a table for them.

B   is also fine. However, the arrangement was not for eight on the dot, but for "around eight," so the chances are that people will not be there.

C   is the option that most Spaniards will choose.

D   is excessively late, since it does not leave enough time to eat and get to the movie.

COMMENT: Eight o' clock is set as a meeting time to allow for flexibility and still leave enough time for the planned activities. This flexibility is signaled by the phrase "sobre las ocho." Once Judy becomes better acquainted with the group, she will know how punctual they tend to be.

Maleducado

Jeff is a professor on a Fulbright scholarship, teaching American literature at a Spanish university. Accustomed to a small private college, he dislikes the crowded, smoky, noisy halls of the university and usually hurries to and from his office as quickly and unobtrusively as possible, speaking to no one. He knew no Spanish prior to coming to Spain, and though he is taking Spanish classes, he does not find the language easy—another reason why he feels shy around groups of Spaniards talking loudly at high speed.

One day Jeff buys a bottle of wine to take to dinner at a friend's house after work and accidentally drops it on the tiled floor of his office. Broken glass flies everywhere and a pool of wine covers the floor. Jeff goes looking for one of the housekeepers to ask her to come and clean up. She is slow to understand what he wants, answers abruptly and keeps him waiting in his office for quite some time before she arrives with her mop and broom. Why?

———————————

Jeff has unwittingly offended many people, including the maintenance staff, by hastening past them without a greeting. He has been labeled a rude (maleducado) and standoffish person. Based on this reputation, the housekeeper is unwilling to help him.

COMMENT: As in many countries where wine is abundant and apparently omnipresent, its use is strictly regulated by custom and convention. A university professor's office is not the place for a bottle of wine. Further, Spaniards have seen enough drunk tourists and alcoholic expatriates to have developed some stereotypes about foreigners and wine. Disapproval on this score may also have influenced the housekeeper's attitude.

The Appointment

Karen, an American student at a language academy in Spain, has an appointment at 10:00 A.M. with the assistant director to discuss the program in general and some upcoming field trips. She should arrive

A. fifteen minutes early.

B. on time.

C. fifteen minutes late.

D. thirty minutes late.

A is the safest option, though being early is not a particular advantage.

B is the most appropriate choice.

C is taking a chance that the assistant director will also be late. If he is not, and if Karen keeps him waiting, she will be perceived as rude.

D is definitely unacceptable.

COMMENT: As in the U.S., professional appointments should be taken seriously. Since Karen is in a position of less authority than the assistant director, she is expected to be on time, though he may be late.

Piropos and Other Forms of Address

Pam is traveling alone by train from Madrid to Santiago de Compostela to take a Spanish course. During her short stay in Madrid since arriving from the U.S., she has already received a number of piropos on the street, and men have pressed against her on the subway. No sooner has the train pulled out than she becomes aware of the steady stares of several men, one of them a well-dressed older man on the seat opposite. Pam should

A. avoid eye contact.

B. move to another seat.

C. try to stare them down.

D. strike up a conversation.

A *is a fairly certain way of forestalling unwanted attention.*

B *is probably the most reliable solution, especially if Pam finds some women to sit with.*

C *will never work. Since staring is not considered rude, someone who is staring cannot be embarrassed by having the stare returned.*

D *could produce a variety of results. On the one hand, Pam might make a friend. On the other, she might find herself in an uncomfortable or potentially dangerous situation if she treats the man as a neutral or protective figure and he takes her to be an easy foreign pickup.*

COMMENT: American women who live in big cities often have a stronger instinct for self-preservation than college students or women who are used to being friendly and outgoing with strangers. For these women, the avoidance tactics described above may be distasteful. However, Pam has already discovered that her appearance marks her as easy prey. Furthermore, an older man may have some outdated ideas about foreign women, and being well dressed is no guarantee of trustworthiness.

118

It's the Rule

Kathy runs the library attached to a United States consulate in Spain. One day a student asks about art schools in the U.S. Kathy recommends a directory listing different schools and colleges, and the student spends several hours looking through it and copying down information. When Kathy starts closing the library for the day, the student asks if she can check out the directory, since she won't be able to visit the library again until next week. Kathy says that according to library policy, reference books cannot be checked out. The student won't take no for an answer. She persists and, in the face of Kathy's repeated refusals, grows indignant and finally demands to see Kathy's supervisor. Kathy loses her patience and says "It's the rule and that's all" and holds the door open. The student leaves, muttering angrily about Americans. How could Kathy have resolved such an encounter more gracefully?

Spanish people are casual about regulations. When dealing with a person, they expect there to be some room for negotiation and react angrily if the person just keeps repeating the regulation.

Kathy would have obtained better results by, first, explaining why the regulation exists—directories are expensive to replace if lost, and the information needs to be readily available to library patrons at all times. Second, she could have discussed the problem from the student's viewpoint—she could come back later, or send a friend or relative tomorrow.

The process of explanation and discussion makes Kathy's refusal much more acceptable. Spaniards say "Hablando, la gente se entiende" (Discussion is the way to understanding). By participating in a discussion, Kathy should be able to forestall both the student's indignation and her own resentment. If all else fails, she should be ready with her supervisor's name. "¿Con quién tengo que hablar?" (Who do I need to talk to?) is a common question from Spaniards who don't get their own way.

Enchufe

John manages a Spanish branch office for an American corporation. A new entry-level position is opening up, and soon after this is announced Antonio, one of the Spanish employees, asks to speak with John. In the course of conversation he mentions a cousin who is interested in the new position and asks John to interview him.

Although the company has no official policy against employing several members of the same family, John feels uncomfortable with the request. People at the American head office have heard and passed on to him some horror stories about nepotism in Spain, and he is anxious to keep his office clean of such insinuations.

John tells Antonio that he would rather not interview his cousin. Antonio does not argue but looks disappointed and offended, and John later notices him in subdued conversation with one or two employees. John is concerned that he may have mishandled the matter. What happened and how could John have handled the situation better?

Antonio made the request out of a sense of family obligation. John's refusal implies that the cousin is not even worth considering, which is offensive to Antonio. Furthermore, Antonio's family may feel that he let his cousin down by not trying hard enough. Finally, John's refusal may have deprived him of an excellent candidate. It would have been better to agree to an interview.

Resources

The following is a brief listing of material available in the U.S. that offers an introduction to Spain or to cross-cultural communication and adaptation.

1. Books

Brenan, Gerald. *The Spanish Labyrinth: An Account of the Social and Political Background of the Spanish Civil War.* New York: Cambridge University Press, 1990.

First published in 1943, this remains one of the classic studies of the Spanish Civil War.

Cohen, David, and Rick Smolan. *A Day in the Life of Spain.* San Francisco: Collins SF, 1988.

Beautiful photographs capture moments in the daily lives of a wide variety of Spaniards in every possible setting. These photographs are especially useful because they record the contemporary scene.

Crow, John A. *Spain: The Root and the Flower.* Berkeley: University of California Press, 1985.

Hooper, John. *The Spaniards: A Portrait of the New Spain.* New York: Viking Penguin, 1987.

John Hooper is an English journalist who spent a number of years as the correspondent in Spain and Portugal for the British daily, *The Guardian.* He has produced a comprehensive and readable study of the transition to democracy after 1975.

Michener, James A. *Iberia: Spanish Travels and Reflections.* New York: Fawcett Crest, 1968.

This is one of James Michener's best known and best loved books. Twenty-five years have rendered much of the social and political commentary obsolete. However, the book is valuable for its combination of history and personal observation, covering twelve distinct cities and regions. Michener's prose is as readable as ever, and his love of Spain is evident on every page.

Kohls, L. Robert. *Survival Kit for Overseas Living.* Yarmouth, ME: Intercultural Press, 1984.

This deceptively slim book explains the basic concepts of culture and cross-cultural adaptation in layman's language, enlivened with guidelines, checklists and exercises.

Storti, Craig. *The Art of Crossing Cultures.* Yarmouth, ME: Intercultural Press, 1990.

Craig Storti presents a model for the process of adapting to another culture. He explains the kinds of adjustments to be made, problems that can arise, and a technique for adapting successfully. This gracefully written book is enhanced with quotations from an array of literary sources.

2. Films

NOTE: The films in this section are sometimes shown in the U.S. at specialty theaters; they are also available on video, subtitled in English.

Almodóvar, Pedro.
Many American are familiar with *Woman on the Verge of a Nervous Breakdown*, which enjoyed great popularity in the U.S. Almodóvar is the most prolific of the current directors, producing a film a year in his characteristic style—zany, sometimes weird, and frequently outrageous. Among his titles are *Dark Habits*, *The Law of Desire*, *Matador*, *What Have I Done to Deserve This?*, *Tie me up! Tie me down!*, *Labyrinth of Passion*, and *High Heels*.Almodóvar, Pedro.

Aragón, Manuel Gutiérrez.
Demons in the Garden (1982) and *Half of Heaven* (1988) are social narratives like Saura's films of the 1970s, but with fewer sinister undercurrents.

Buñuel, Luis.
The father of modern Spanish cinema first made his name with the surreal *Un chien andalou*. He worked from exile in France and many of his films were banned in Spain. His only film currently available in the U.S. is *Viridiana* (1961).

Erice, Victor.
Erice directed *The Spirit of the Beehive* (1973), a lyrical portrait of childhood and traditional village life.

Saura, Carlos.

Saura was one of the most prolific and influential directors of the 1970s. Films such as *The Garden of Delights* (1970), *Cría Cuervos* (1977) and *Mama Turns 100* (1979) chronicle family and social relationships. In the 1980s Saura made his "Dance Trilogy" in collaboration with the Antonio Gades flamenco dance troupe: *Carmen*, based on the Bizet opera; *Blood Wedding*, based on the play by Federico García Lorca; and *El Amor Brujo*, based on music by Manuel de Falla. In 1991 Saura took another turn with *Ay, Carmela!* about a group of traveling musicians during the Civil War.

Glossary

Words

abrazo: hug (*un abrazo:* informal ending for letters)
adiós: good-bye/go with God
ahora: now
allioli: garlic mayonnaise
ambiente: atmosphere
apertura: liberalization; literally "opening"
beso: kiss (*un besos:* informal ending for letters—women only)
buenos días: good morning
buenas tardes: good afternoon
castellano: Castilian; also Latin American variety of Spanish language
catedrático: tenured professor
cava: Catalan champagne
civismo: good citizenship
colegio oficial: official college or professional society
comité de empresa: employees' council
confianza: trust (*una persona de confianza:* one who can be trusted)
convenio: job agreement
detallismo: detail consciousness/*el prolijo detallismo de los americanos:* the Americans' unlimited passion for details

el vicio español: the Spanish vice
enchufe: contacts
envidia: jealousy, envy
escándalo público: public scandal
Estatuto del trabajador: Workers' Code
familia: family
familia política: in-laws
ganster: gangster
gansterismo: lawlessness
hablando fuerte: talking loudly
hacer el ridículo: to look foolish
Hacienda: the Spanish Treasury
hidalgo: literally, the son of somebody; a gentleman
hola: hello
horario de verano: summer schedule
insolidario: lacking in solidarity
jefe de estación: stationmaster
la madre patria: the mother country
Levante: Mediterranean coast
ley: law
machismo: male sexist behavior
machista: male chauvinist
maleducado: boorish, bad mannered
mañana: tomorrow
menú del día: daily special
meseta: high plateau
mili: military service
natural de…: native of...
pasatiempo: pastime
pícaro: rascal
pijo: spoiled rich kid
piropo: compliment or comment about appearance
portero: doorman
reglamento: the section of Spanish legislation specifying details
    accompanying certain laws
Reyes Católicos: Catholic Monarchs

señora: title for a married or older woman
señorita: title for an unmarried or younger woman
sevillanas: a type of Andalucían dance
suecas: Swedes
suerte: luck
tapas: varied snacks to accompany drinks
tertulia: circle of friends, typically men, who meet regularly in
    the same bar or restaurant
tú: informal form of "you"
urbanización: modern housing development
usted: polite form of "you"

Expressions

Aqui hay blancos, negritos, y negritos con cualificaciones: In this
    company there are white folks, darkies, and darkies with
    qualifications
Club de Futbol Barcelona: the Barcelona Soccer Association
¿Con quién tengo que hablar?: Who do I need to talk to?
Es igual: It's all the same
Faci d' Alcalde: You Be the Mayor
Faltar al respeto: to be lacking in respec
Haberlo dicho hombre: Why didn't you say something before?
Hablando, la gente se entiende: Discussion is the way to under-
    standing
Hecha la ley, hecha la trampa: Every law has its loophole
Ir al grano: to get to the point
més que un club: more than a club
No hay nadie en la calle: There's nobody about
Obedezco, pero no cumplo: I obey but do not comply
OTAN No—Bases Fuera: No to NATO—Out with the bases
Prohibido cantar: No singing
¿Qué hacemos?: What shall we do?
¿Quiere tomar algo?: Would you like to have something (to
    drink)?

Respeten el descanso de los vecinos: Respect the sleep of our neighbors

Sobre las ocho: at around 8:00

Somos comodones: We like things easy

Somos el vagón de la cola: We always bring up the rear

Son apagados, pero van haciendo: They're very low-key, but they get on with the job

Te invito: You're my guest

Trata de dormir seis horas: Make a point of getting six hours' sleep

Un día es un día: Live for today

Vive de tus padres hasta que puedas vivir de tus hijos: Live off your parents until you can live off your children

Vivimos en comunidad: We're a community

Ya me lo pagará mañana: You can pay me tomorrow

Ya nos conocemos: We know each other

Endnotes

[1] Diaz-Plaja, Fernando. *The Spaniard and the Seven Deadly Sins*. London: Pan Books, 1971, [page 211]. Originally published in Spanish as *El español y los siete pecados capitales*. Madrid: Alianza Editorial, 23rd ed. 1986.

[2] Ibid., [page 56-7].

[3] Hooper, John. *The Spaniards, A Portrait of the New Spain*. New York: Viking Penguin, 1987, [page 189].

[4] Punset, Eduardo. "Porqué no innovan los españoles." *El País*, November 8, 1986.

[5] Peters, Thomas J., and Robert H. Waterman, Jr. *In Search of Excellence: Lessons from America's Best-Run Companies*. New York: Harper & Row, 1982.

[6] McCaffrey, James A., and Craig R. Haffner. "When Two Cultures Collide: Doing Business Overseas." *Training and Development Journal*, October 1985 [pages 26-31].

[7] Fountaine, Margaret. *Love among the Butterflies*. Harmondsworth, Middlesex: Penguin Books, 1982, [page 169].

[8] Diaz-Plaja. *The Spaniard and the Seven Deadly Sins* [page 91].